Elizabeth Strong Worthington

The Biddy Club

And how its members, wise and otherwise, some toughened and some tenderfooted in the rugged ways of housekeeping, grappled with the troublous servant question, to the great advantage of themselves, and, as they hope, of many others

Elizabeth Strong Worthington

The Biddy Club
And how its members, wise and otherwise, some toughened and some tenderfooted in the rugged ways of housekeeping, grappled with the troublous servant question, to the great advantage of themselves, and, as they hope, of many others

ISBN/EAN: 9783337084592

Printed in Europe, USA, Canada, Australia, Japan

Cover: Foto ©ninafisch / pixelio.de

More available books at **www.hansebooks.com**

THE BIDDY CLUB: AND HOW ITS MEMBERS, WISE AND OTHERWISE, SOME TOUGHENED AND SOME TENDER-FOOTED IN THE RUGGED WAYS OF HOUSEKEEPING, GRAPPLED WITH THE TROUBLOUS SERVANT QUESTION, TO THE GREAT ADVANTAGE OF THEMSELVES, AND, AS THEY HOPE, OF MANY OTHERS.

By

GRIFFITH A. NICHOLAS.

CHICAGO:
A. C. McCLURG AND COMPANY.
1888.

COPYRIGHT
BY A. C. MCCLURG AND COMPANY.
A.D. 1887.

TABLE OF CONTENTS.

CHAPTER I.

                                                                       PAGE

WHY AND HOW THE CLUB WAS FORMED . . . 13

CHAPTER II.

SOME PERSONALITIES 23

CHAPTER III.

A YOUNG HOUSEKEEPER'S EXPERIENCES.

Training of mistresses. — A few weeks' apprenticeship 34

CHAPTER IV.

SELECTING AND MANAGING SERVANTS.

Kitchen conveniences. — Kind of servant to avoid. — Servants' dress. — Servants' time out. — Order of work. — Preparation for Sunday. — Easy suppers. — Children's diet. — Table service. — Serving of meals. — Servants replacing dishes they break. — How to select a good servant. — Servants' uniform . . 51

CHAPTER V.

SOME DIFFICULT PROBLEMS.

Servants' personal care. — Independence in matter of rules. — Good servants in preference to expensive dress or handsome furniture. — A popular fallacy on the subject of motherly devotion. — Training a nurse. — The needs of older children 73

CHAPTER VI.

SCIENTIFIC HOUSEKEEPING.

Political and domestic economy. — Hamerton on diet. — How to avert some housekeeping troubles. — How to economize intelligently. — An inexpensive table. — Recipes for salads. — A pretty dish . . 90

CHAPTER VII.

MONEY MATTERS.

Woman's rights in financial affairs. — Ante-nuptial arrangements. — Partnership. — Distinction between a gift and the right by earning. — A moneyed arrangement. — Another family's way. — Proper steps to take. — Small men. — Husband and wife equal partners. — The "Nation" on the liability of a woman 104

CHAPTER VIII.

THE SERVANTS' SIDE.

Teaching a servant system. — Servants' evenings. — Mistresses to blame for most of the present evils. — Hours of servants' labor. — Wages. — Board. — Beecher on slavery. — Graded wages. — Plan for people of small means. — Skilled service. — Pay for women who work by the day or job. — Increasing wages. — Understanding when engaging a servant 125

CHAPTER IX.

SERVANTS' LEISURE TIME.

Servants' objection to living out from town. — Night work. — Evenings at home. — Servants' company. — Their leisure absolutely theirs. — When mistresses become the slaves of their servants . . . 145

CHAPTER X.

HONOR ABOVE AND BELOW STAIRS.

Article on shop-girls. — Caste. — Mistaken ideas of foreigners relative to caste in America. — A lesson on caste. — Laxity in keeping promises. — Significance of a contract. — Where girls can find a home and earn moderate wages. — Dishonorable mistresses. — Searching a servant's trunk. — Trying to save a dishonest servant . . 153

CHAPTER XI.

BRAINS IN HOUSEKEEPING.

Perfect servants. — Choice of faults. — Good housekeeping brain-work. — System. — How to learn system. — Proper care of children. — Proper clothing. — Little girls' exercise. — Outline of a busy systematic day. — Keeping children healthy. — Wasting time and strength on calls. — Children trained to make trouble. — Social duties to one's neighbors. — Emerson on length of calls. — How to make the most of time. — Delightful social evenings 173

CHAPTER XII.

A MOTHER'S RIGHTS AND DUTIES.

"The Sad Fortunes of the Reverend Amos Barton." — How Dickens paints wrongs. — "Spectator" on unnecessary sacrifice. — A mother's duty toward other women in training her sons. — Over-population a problem of the near future. — The burial of a talent. — A union of heart and brains. — Women chiefly responsible. — Public schools 191

CHAPTER XIII.

METHODS OF HOME GOVERNMENT.

A thorough understanding. — Praise as an instrument of government. — Awing servants. — How to avoid impertinence. — How to call out impertinence. — Occasions for discipline. — Improvement of servants' character. — A Southern lady's way 204

CHAPTER XIV.

CARE FOR SERVANTS' CHARACTER.

PAGE

Servants' vacations. — Co-partnership. — Developing self-respect. — Making economy dignified. — "Stylish" extravagance. — Untruthful servants. — Slow servants. — Religious training. — Narrowness in theology. — Love and liberty 222

CHAPTER XV.

HOMES, NOT HOUSES.

Various kinds of conversation. — The great within the small. — Keeping homes, not houses. — Of what women do not talk. — Along the lake-shore. — Home 236

CHAPTER XVI.

SERVANTS' TABLES, WITH AN INTERRUPTION.

Servants' tables. — Uninterrupted meals. — Good cold dinner dishes for summer. — Sitting-room for servants. — Servants objects for charitable work. — Servants' bedroom. — Children's need to be incited to good conduct. — " North American Review " on Practical Penology. — Effect of the servant trouble on people at large. — A broken man. — Finding work. — A lady-like accomplishment. 248

CHAPTER XVII.

SIMPLIFYING LIFE.

PAGE

Simplifying life. — Diminishing the burdens of married life. — Behind the age. — " Our Country " on intemperance. — A flexible system. — Capacity for management. — Idle chattering. — A well-ordered family. — Practical knowledge. — Mingling of kindness and dignity. — Hard features of a servant's work. — Overburdened wives and mothers. — Gasoline ranges 270

CHAPTER XVIII.

ONE THING AT A TIME.

Concentration of thought and aim. — Recipe for preserving youth and health. — Policy of treating servants well. — Convalescence. — Sympathy from servants. — Rewarding servants. — Servants' Christmas. — Great beauty at small expense. — Motion to adjourn 286

CHAPTER XIX.

SOME GOOD RESOLUTIONS.

Laxity in the last meeting. — Value of a good servant. — Vote of thanks. — Effect of Club . . . 300

THE BIDDY CLUB.

THE BIDDY CLUB.

CHAPTER I.

WHY AND HOW IT WAS FORMED.

I WAS sitting in my study one spring morning, suffering from that state of depression which generally follows undue exhilaration. This depression was not without real cause, as will be understood when I say that I held in my hand a rejected manuscript. I had built an airy castle upon this article, which was an attempt to prove that it was not an apple, but a banana, upon which Adam and Eve so sinfully lunched. I thought the essay both original and spicy, and expected others to agree with me; therefore when, from an editor whom I had accounted my friend, I received mine own again, coupled with a letter asking me to forego such nonsense in the future and write something worth printing, I naturally sank into a state best described as low in my mind. While I was occupied with some gloomy reflections upon the subject of my ill-luck, and some scornful ones on the subject of stupid and indiscriminating editors, I heard Dolly's light step near the door.

"A kingdom for your pen!" she exclaimed, entering the room.

"A fig for my pen!" I answered contemptuously, and then added, in disrespectful reference to the unhappy manuscript, "A banana for my pen!"

"What is the matter?" she asked. "Have Adam and Eve returned?"

I gloomily nodded my head.

"They must want a spring suit," said Dolly.

"They'll get nothing from me, — not so much as a shoe-string," I answered, thrusting the luckless couple into a drawer of my desk and turning the key upon them.

"Never mind, Griff," said Dolly. "It isn't Adam you care for, nor yet Eve; at least, I hope it's not Eve."

She paused and looked at me anxiously, but I assured her I didn't care any more for the lady in question than the editor had cared for her; and nothing could be smaller than his esteem.

"Well, then," she continued, "I think I can help you. You care for success, don't you?"

I admitted I was not indifferent to it, and averred I saw no reason why success did not immediately follow the writing of such an article as that.

"I am afraid," said Dolly, anxiously, "that the public in general is not so deeply interested in its great-grandparents as it ought to be."

"Well, what subject would you consider more interesting, pray?" I asked, by way of giving expression to a certain testiness of feeling, rather than from any desire to seek information.

"Why, several, — the children here, for instance; the servants; the household in general."

"Dolly," I said, "do try to be practical." I instinctively felt that I was upon the brink of defeat, and so assumed a tone of masculine superiority and manfully evaded the issue.

"I'll make an effort," she answered good-naturedly. "But, to return to the subject, I want to accomplish a certain work, and I need a pen; now, you write —"

"Oh, yes, I write, and I'm written to!" I said, glancing savagely at the editor's letter.

"Well, I'll give you a subject that will serve us both; for if I mistake not, you'll achieve success with it, and I will —"

"What am I to write about?" I interrupted.

"Servants first, and afterward children."

"Dolly," I said with emphasis, "I won't do it! I utterly refuse to chain my Pegasus to a plough."

"Why, you've just been writing a domestic

letter telling what Adam and Eve had to eat! I really think this is a step upward,— to treat of human beings apart from their food."

I had nothing more to say, and I picked up my pen with weary disgust.

"Come," I said, apostrophizing it; "Pegasus is too much of a name, if you're going to write of Biddies and Babies. Old Peg will do for you now."

"Don't be so scornful, if you please," said Dolly; "I am honoring you by asking your aid in a great undertaking. I want to establish associations all over the United States, and I'll —"

I threw down my pen.

"Dolly!" I exclaimed, "you know that a man feels dilapidated anyhow this spring weather, and it's nothing less than cowardice for you to take advantage of his weakness, and come at him with a rolling-pin in the shape of a universal association."

Dolly laughed, but failed to withdraw.

"If you'll let me," she said, "I'll explain. I think we women have talked over our servants in an aimless, gossipy way long enough, and it's time we talked to some purpose. I've thought so for months, but more especially since paying a visit to Mrs. Hughes last week. We were speaking of this servant-girl trouble, and she remarked, 'I don't think we women are very smart, or we would have combined long ago and found some way to lessen these annoyances.' Now, what I want to bring about is this very combination."

"In other words, you wish to start a club," I said.

"Oh, no, Griff; be merciful! We've had enough of that! I sometimes think we must be the most immoral people here, for we have been all but clubbed to death this winter. I've been such a sufferer from this that even the sight of a twig now causes my bones to ache and my flesh to tremble."

"What do you propose to call your association, pray?"

"Why, nothing; I don't want it to be anything like a club, for I 'm sick of electing officers and being asked to vote yea or nay, — which generally means yea, whether you want to or not; and as to voting by ballot — I won't have it."

"Well, what part am I to play in this nameless assemblage?"

"Why, you hold the pen of a ready writer — "

"And you doubtless think the pen is mightier than the sword, — or, in other words, the feminine tongue!"

"Put it any way you like, just so you sound

our voice all over the Union," said Dolly, who seemed ready to make all possible concessions in order to gain her end.

"I suppose," I observed, "that if I am expected to do that, the association will be generous enough to furnish me a speaking-trumpet — at my own expense!"

"Come, Griff," Dolly remonstrated, "don't be frivolous; this is serious business. Bear in mind, sir, that all future beefsteaks, waffles, and corn-fritters depend largely upon the success of these meetings."

"In that case," I said, resuming my discarded pen, "I am ready for work; but would you kindly, madam, be a trifle more explicit as to my task?"

"Why, I thought I told you that you were to write an account of our meetings. You are to be our honored secretary."

"Dolly," I exclaimed, "it is quite clear to me that, however delicately you may endeavor to disguise the unsavory truth, I am in this affair to be but a tool! Now, my dear madam, I wish respectfully to demand of you the kind of tool I am expected to personate. If you confess it is a gimlet, I decline; for however marked my abilities may be in that direction, I refuse to exercise them in boring this noble assemblage."

But Dolly was a woman, and she proceeded to

soothe and flatter and coax, until she had me just where she wanted, and I made all sorts of ridiculous concessions. Having thus committed myself, as far as my line of conduct was concerned, there was no help for me, and I passively awaited further developments.

That very afternoon Dolly donned her best and sallied forth in quest of victims for me. I merely put the matter so to save my dignity. I know, as well as anybody, that I was the victimized.

Near tea-time she returned, and ran up to my study in high spirits.

"They're all coming," she said.

"Of course they are!" I responded. "If that's all ye went out for to see, I could have saved you the trouble. I knew they'd all come."

"Now, Griff, don't be fierce. You must keep amiable, whatever happens, for I feel as if the success of this venture depended largely upon you."

I swallowed this luscious morsel and smiled.

"Have you any specific plan of action for to-morrow?" I inquired, in tones of unrippled trust and belief.

"Oh, yes! I rely upon Mrs. Hughes to be my main speaker. She is really the best qualified, for she regulates her household and her time wonderfully."

The mention of Mrs. Hughes's name as a leading member of the coming body changed my amiability from a spurious to a genuine quantity; for I greatly admired the lady. Although she made no noise about the matter, she was nevertheless known and looked up to as the best of wives, mothers, and housekeepers. Her husband always had the appearance of a man well fed, well sewed, and otherwise well off. It was said, and I could readily believe the report, that his wife had done much, by her able home-management, to build him up financially, from a state of "uncomfortably" to a state of "comfortably off." Besides possessing all domestic virtues, Mrs. Hughes was very attractive, a charming hostess, — well, in short, excepting only my Dolly, the prettiest, most interesting woman I knew. She had one advantage over Dolly, in that she was older; and so, having had more experience, was more competent to teach. I would, however, lay a large wager that my little woman would be her equal at her age.

"I tried, Griff," said Dolly, "to put the matter in such a light that all I asked would come. You know some ladies don't like to confess to having trouble with their servants. So I told them we wanted all who had anything to say or to learn on that subject, to be present to-morrow."

"You've built a broad platform, I must say; I think it will hold them all."

"That's what I thought," said Dolly, her bright face fairly glowing with pleasure. "I asked Mrs. Hughes to come and teach us, but she was very modest about it. She was not silly, however, for she admitted that her longer experience had probably given her something of value to impart to younger housekeepers; but she also said she felt she had much to learn, and would be glad of an opportunity to listen to the opinions of others on the subject."

"Dolly," I said, "you must speak with wit and wisdom to-morrow, if you wish me to act as your scribe."

"Oh, Griff, I can't!" she protested, laughing. "I once heard of a lady who became so marvellously witty that she could even talk about the weather engagingly; and the cause of all this brilliancy was merely a half-hour given each night, before retiring, to the reading of some author famous either for his wit or his style. I tried this for several weeks, in hopes I could deal handsomely with this servant-girl question; but I decided the subject was beyond help."

Secretly, however, I believed that Dolly had not given up the matter as hopeless, but was still struggling with it. I noticed that she wore an occupied air that evening, and I averred the next morning that I distinctly heard her attempt two feeble jokes in her sleep, and I was quite positive she was wrestling with Owen Meredith's immortal lines on "pining" and "dining" when the rising-bell rudely interrupted her.

CHAPTER II.

SOME PERSONALITIES.

THE next afternoon, at three o'clock, our door-bell began ringing with great vigor; nor did it cease until ten ladies had gained admittance. With the exception of Mrs. Hughes and two others, there was nothing so very unusual about this gathering. One of these two was a lady of uncertain age and position. It was supposed that her husband controlled a good business, but that, owing to her extravagance, they had nothing laid up, and indeed were at times pinched beyond a point that was pleasant. This lady had in some hapless moment acquired the acquaintance of Mrs. Leaders and Mrs. Van Styke, the wives of two of the wealthiest men in the city, and it seemed her one aim in life to have it thought she lived as they lived, and also that she was on terms of the closest intimacy with them. Rarely could one converse with her for ten minutes without hearing something of Mrs. Leaders's opinion of the weather, or Mrs. Van Styke's health. A friend of ours, upon hearing that this lady had called, would always ask his wife, in a tone of deep solicitude, —

"And how is Mrs. Van Styke?"

I would not wish to paint this lady in too glaring colors. She was not loud, she was not obtrusive. In many ways she was agreeable, even interesting; but she had her little peculiarities, and these were known and smiled at among her acquaintances. As I wish to avoid mentioning names in this narrative, I will designate this inoffensive lady as the Imitation Millionnaire.

The other individual whom I wish to describe was a lady whom Dolly and I had known before our or her marriage. She had been one of those girls who, without any particular strength or individuality, possess a strong power of attraction, — an attraction which is possibly to be at once explained and rendered more mysterious by the word magnetic. She was a passive rather than an active character; gentle, quiet, yet capable of enjoying her rather remarkable capacity for winning and holding captives. Few girls could have had more lovers than she, and from out them all she chose a man who in character was directly opposed to her, — abrupt, decisive, active, energetic, intellectual within a very prescribed limit. I should have said that he chose her rather than she him, for it was whispered at the time that she did not really fall in love with him, but rather gave way before his decisive wooing. Immediately after their marriage he took her to another city, where he engaged in business for himself, and she was seen no more by her old friends for five years. At the end of that time he brought her back, but so changed that no one would have known her. Her pretty, gentle beauty was a thing of the past. Indeed, I could never see her without recalling some wild flowers I once plucked in the woods. They were cool with dew-drops, — so pretty and fresh-looking, — but I drove some miles farther, holding them in my hand, and when I reached home their beauty and freshness were gone. I sprinkled them with water, laid them in a cool dark room, but with no avail; their spirit was broken, and nothing I could do would tempt them to lift their pretty heads again. I was haunted all that morning with a feeling that I had taken some innocent, gentle creature away from the home it loved, and its heart had broken. I never had such a feeling toward cultivated flowers. When this pale, quiet-faced lady returned, it took us some time to recognize her; and when we did, and rallied around her with our greetings, she showed but little interest in her old friends. Her husband, too, seemed changed. His activity and energy were centred on his business. He had a fretful, peevish way of looking at life. His favorite theme was the amount required for necessary expenditures, and the high price of various articles of food and clothing. In his business he had been both successful and unsuccessful; he was still able to go on for himself, but he had seen reverses and had worked very hard. I have no doubt that his family was somewhat extravagant; for although no one could look at his wife and accuse her of spending money on any pleasures, yet from what I know of her character I am positive she could not have been a good manager. She lacked both the intellect and the energy; but any man of sense could have told that when she was a girl. She and her husband, with their family of three children, settled in one of two pleasant houses. Their home was comfortably furnished, and they kept two servants. This latter expense, I was told, was one of his favorite themes. He was constantly telling his wife of all the women he knew who kept but one servant or none at all; but she took these remarks quietly, as she did everything else he said. Her attitude toward him was quite a study. She did not seem in the least afraid of him, nor yet utterly indifferent. I can only describe her as hopeless, broken. Some might have called him a home man, but

I disliked him so thoroughly that I always attributed his constant presence at the domestic hearth to the fact that he was not wanted anywhere else. As far as known, he never made any effort to be agreeable to the girl whom he had shut off from life by marrying her. We often looked in upon them, through their half-open shutters, as we passed; he was always reading a newspaper and she was always sewing. Sometimes he was sitting with his back to her. No one who went to the house ever heard him address an endearing word to her, still less demonstrate the slightest affection in other ways. Once when she was dressed in a heavy cloak she asked him to draw on her rubbers for her. He had a child on his knee at the time, and he reminded her of this, and asked why she did n't put them on herself. It was said by one or two who, through pity, went there frequently, that she made pathetic attempts to improve her housekeeping, and to set a frugal and attractive table; but no matter what she did, there was always something left undone, and this last he never failed to notice, though he was seemingly blind to the first. The next-door neighbors used to say that they could hear his voice every night, going twang, twang, twang, like an ill-conditioned jew's-harp; but they never heard her reply to his complaints.

Dolly was much surprised when this lady consented to attend her meeting, for she had not supposed she would take any interest in it. She told Dolly, however, that if she came she must do so without speaking to her husband on the subject, for he could not bear the mention of anything of the kind; he thought women ought to stay at home and take care of their houses and children, instead of gadding about and gossiping with one another. Dolly tried to impress on her mind the fact that this meeting was not intended to encourage or even countenance gossip; it was called for the purpose of having women meet and discuss the best mode of governing their servants, and learn from such discussions what in justice they ought to grant to those in their service, and also what it was proper to expect and to require of them. She seemed to allow all this herself, but said that her husband could never be brought to view the meetings in any such light. He detested the very mention of everything of the kind; in his mind it was all associated with woman's rights, strong-mindedness, literary pretensions, and all else that was worthless and unwomanly.

"I could n't say anything more after that," said Dolly, in repeating the conversation to me; "one can't speak against a woman's husband to her, so I just laughingly urged her to come and see for herself that we were not vicious or in any way dangerous. I hope that old narrow-minded tyrant won't learn of it and keep her at home; it would do her good to get away from those children and that everlasting sewing for a while, even if there was no more to gain."

I said nothing, but I sympathized with Dolly in her dislike of that man. In fact, I never saw his wife, with her white, lifeless face, without having a strong inclination to knock him down. But as he was much larger and more muscular than myself, I always remembered that anger was sinful, and restrained it just in time.

The first subject that was to come up in Dolly's meeting was that of my presence. Dolly and I had already debated this matter in private. I told her the ladies might not be willing to speak freely if I was in the room; and as it was necessary that I should hear what was going on, in order to write a lifelike account of it, I suggested that I should place myself near a certain register, where I could hear without being heard or seen. This quite shocked Dolly's sense of honor; but I maintained that Howells's admirable little comedy had rendered such a situation quite respectable, even classic. As Dolly refused to listen to any such argument, there was nothing further to do but lay the matter before the ladies. I being the matter, I naturally felt some sensitiveness as to the manner in which I was laid before so august an assemblage, and begged Dolly to use tenderness tempered with discretion. This she promised to do; and as soon as the last lady was seated, she opened the subject by remarking that she felt sure that, however widely they might differ upon some points, they would agree that all over the United States there was a call for the establishment of some sort of system in the management of servants. This remark being received with a murmur of assent, Dolly was emboldened to add that she was confident all the ladies gathered there would join her in an attempt to aid the thousands of mistresses who were careworn by reason of trouble with their service. Another murmur of assent, albeit less decided, encouraged Dolly to remind the ladies of what they already knew, — that her husband was a contributor to a number of magazines and papers. Some of the ladies, seeing the drift of this remark, refused to murmur any longer; but Dolly was quite highly wrought up by this time, and went on regardless of support. She briefly said she wanted her husband to write a little account of the forming of a club for the purpose of mending domestic service (Dolly ought to have put this under the head of Civil Service Reform), and that in order that he might do so intelligently, she wished him to know how they proceeded. Of course, Dolly hastened to say, he would give no names, and indeed he would disguise the whole matter completely, so that no one need feel she was made conspicuous. It was only necessary that he should have some groundwork for his articles. She was sure no one would object, since what he wrote might be the means of establishing similar clubs all over the Union, and doing endless good.

("That is," — I said mentally, for I was somewhere in the vicinity of that register, in spite of Dolly, — "that is, if his articles are accepted by that very narrow-minded and pig-headed person the editor.")

Dolly was interrupted here by a volley from the assemblage.

"Oh, we never could say anything worth hearing if your husband were present!" said one, whose voice I recognized as belonging to a certain frivolous acquaintance of ours. A quick doubt flashed through my brain as to whether, even in my absence, her remarks would quite equal Solomon's.

"Let him come," said another; "if he can stand it, we ought to."

I laughed at this speech; it came from a sprightly young married lady, a great favorite of mine, bright as she was pretty.

"Oh, no, we can't have him; it would spoil everything, we'd feel so constrained."

I could not recognize the source of this remark, but I knew it was Mrs. Hughes who spoke next.

"I see no objection; I don't think he's likely to be critical, for he knows we are gathered here to learn, and if, through his coming, others might be benefited, I should be very glad to have him present."

Here I made a mental note to the effect that Mrs. Hughes was, as I had always supposed her, a lady of rare sense.

"We'll have to vote on it," said a voice I did not recognize.

"It ought to be by ballot," said another unknown one.

Unable to help herself, poor Dolly was drawn into the vortex, and in spite of her determination not to vote at all, least of all by ballot, was heard by the register to tear and distribute bits of paper. The vote stood six in favor against five opposed, and upon this slender majority I was admitted, feeling myself in but slim demand, and my seat in the house consequently insecure. There was afterward a sort of compromise made, it being agreed that I should remove myself (I refuse to put it in the passive voice) to an adjacent library, where I might hear without being seen.

"And we'll try to forget all about you," said the Frivolous Young Woman, as I was bidding the company a touching farewell.

"Oh, no; don't let us exert ourselves to do that," said the Sprightly Lady.

CHAPTER III.

A YOUNG HOUSEKEEPER'S EXPERIENCE.

As soon as I was well out of the way, Dolly opened the meeting by saying that perhaps it would be best to call upon some one of the ladies to give an account of her housekeeping experiences, the others making comments or asking questions, as they chose. Dolly was very adroit; she had already decided upon Mrs. Hughes, but she thought best to lead the other ladies to mention her. She knew they would not fail to do this, as she was much liked. Her tact was rewarded by having Mrs. Hughes immediately and unanimously chosen as the one to address the others.

The lady began, not by saying that she was taken by surprise, or was embarrassed by their choice, but by remarking that her husband had often laughingly accused her of being proud of her failures, because she made such haste to expose them to others; but she was of the opinion that we were as frequently benefited by the failures as by the successes of our fellow-beings, and that, having fallen into certain pits herself, she was more than eager to keep others out of them, even though she were obliged to light herself, as it were, in order to warn them.

"When I went to housekeeping," the lady continued, "I knew no more than most American girls; and so far from being ashamed of my ignorance, I was wont to make a jest of it. I used to say that if ever I owned a kitchen it should bear this motto: 'Where ignorance is bliss, 't is folly to be wise.' I remember a gentleman friend suggesting that I should have this printed in Latin or Greek, as in plain legible English it might have a demoralizing effect upon my maidservants. You may think I knew even less than most girls, when I tell you that after I was married I went to the butcher's one morning and ordered a piece of stuffed veal. I have always admired the self-control of the man who waited upon me. I am confident he struggled with an inclination to tell me I scarcely need buy calf, as I evidently had goose enough on hand to last a season. I had a foolish feeling that there was something pretty about ignorance. I found I became very popular with my Irish cook when I showed her that I knew nothing about her department. Each morning, before starting out upon my marketing, I would ask her all sorts of questions as to what I should buy, how much, and so on; but it seemed to me that no matter how well furnished with information I might be before starting, that arch-fiend the butcher would invariably bring me to confusion on some trifling point before I left his shop. Despite this little trouble, however, all seemed to go merrily; and I found housekeeping both easy and pleasant, until a larger trouble appeared, in the shape of my husband's dissatisfaction. When the first glamour of our new relations had somewhat died away, and the romantic had become tinged with the practical, my husband began to realize that the very small sum he had laid up to begin upon had all but melted away; he realized, furthermore, that although he worked very hard we were living beyond our income, with a fair prospect of debt in the future. He found, also, that while there were others whose expenses were as heavy as ours, yet some of our friends, who had as large an income and family as we, were living for much less. It was a great annoyance to me, that just as I was becoming very popular with my Irish cook I found myself losing popularity with my husband. He had a number of plain talks with me on the housekeeping subject, and fortunately I had sense enough to see the truth of his remarks and realize the danger of our situation, though I must allow that I was inwardly nettled, and wished retrenchment were unnecessary. For all that, however, I set myself about it earnestly; but I found I was undertaking a great deal. The moment I attempted to look into the kitchen more closely, my cook grew sulky, and finally said she did not think she was pleasing me as well as she used to, and gave me notice. (She should have said I was not pleasing her as well as I had done.) This roused the woman within me, for I saw I was not mistress of my own house. I let this woman go, and determined to control the next servant, instead of being petted and controlled by her."

"Now comes the tug of war," observed the Sprightly Lady.

"Yes, indeed!" said Mrs. Hughes. "It was June when my Irish cook dismissed me, and before September I had had fifteen servants. None of them were especially vicious, but there was always something wrong. I had sick girls, homesick girls, incompetent girls. It seemed as if each one left my house in a little worse condition than the last; and both my husband and myself became so disheartened that in the fall we broke up housekeeping and went to boarding. As we had a little child and a nurse, we found this a very unsatisfactory way to live; but I had the rest I needed, and a time for most profitable thought, which I also needed. Although my husband was too kind and charitable to say anything, I could not help knowing that secretly he felt I had failed to do my part. I felt so myself, and could not be happy until I had determined to try again. While in this mood I had some conversation with a friend, — an English lady. I was making complaint of the miserable class of servants with which housekeepers had to deal, and I said, 'Don't you think we ought to establish a training-school for them?' She paused a moment, and then replied very earnestly, 'My dear, first of all we need a training-school for mistresses.' To tell the truth, I mentally resented this, regarding it as an imputation against myself.

"When I went to housekeeping again, I found that my experiences had not been without avail. I understood character better, and so could make a wiser choice of servants than formerly. I kept careful accounts, and tried to look after my kitchen closely; but I still had more or less trouble. I changed servants often, kept increasing the wages I paid, and arranged my work in various ways in my efforts to have matters run more smoothly. But I had not yet gone to the root of the matter.

"One evening, in talking with my husband, I mentioned a new clerk he had engaged, and he remarked that although the boy was ignorant, he was so bright and anxious to learn that he would soon be valuable. 'There is nothing,' he said, 'from A to Z, in that office, that I cannot teach him. I have had practical knowledge of it all.' Then he added, rather unnecessarily, I thought at the time: 'When you housekeepers know your business as thoroughly as I know mine, you'll have less trouble with servants.'

The same feeling of resentment which I had experienced when the English lady spoke, sprang up in my heart again, and I saw fit to begin talking about the weather. Not long after that my cook asked me for an increase of pay. She did not think, she said, she could do my work unless she had more. I was already giving her good wages, and my heart died within me as she spoke, for I foresaw another change. Personally this girl was very agreeable to me; she had a pleasant, obliging disposition, and gentle, respectful manners. She was a fairly good cook, and since her coming I had hoped, from week to week, that she would master her work; but she was always behindhand. The ironing was late, the baking hurried, and the scrubbing often omitted. Every day I felt as if I were pushing a great load, and although the girl seemed to try, she never caught up. Every evening until ten she toiled, and still much was left undone.

She said the work was very hard, but she liked me so much she would do it for higher wages. I half decided to pay these rather than change again, but I told her I would think the matter over for a day. My conscience was stirred. I felt I was then paying all I could afford; I felt, too, that my work was not worth more, as wages went. I had but two children, and kept a nurse, who was assisting the cook more than I really felt I ought to let her. I thought over many things, and came to some new conclusions. It was then that I first felt the force of my friend's and my husband's remarks. I went into the kitchen the next day and said, 'Maggie, I have decided that it is not because of the work that we are always behind here, but because of the worker. You do not know how to systematize matters. Now, I know very little about all this myself, but I have resolved to learn. I am coming out into the kitchen to-day to begin, and when I have learned I am going to teach a girl. Now, I like you very much, and would be glad to have you stay; but I am not willing to pay you more until you know more. If you wish to remain and learn of me as I become able to teach you, I will continue to you the same wages, although I consider them very high for a girl who is not thoroughly competent. Think it over yourself, Maggie, and you will see the fault cannot lie in the work. The family is small, the house convenient, and my nurse helps you a great deal.'"

"Did she take all this?" asked the Sprightly Lady.

"Oh, yes. I spoke very kindly. I told her that I wished to talk with her as one woman with another; that I was discouraged because my work did not go better, when I was paying more than I ought to, and making every effort to help matters along. She admitted that possibly the fault lay in herself, and agreed to try another week and see what could be done. And so I began my education."

"You don't mean to say that you went to doing kitchen work when you were n't obliged to!" exclaimed the Frivolous Young Person.

"I certainly did; and I was ashamed that I had not begun before."

"Well, that's more than I'd do! I let my servants attend to their own business, and when they get into a muddle I leave them to get out of it as best they can."

"That sounds like an interesting method," said Mrs. Hughes, courteously; but I could detect a slight shade of irony in her voice. "It's only defect is, that when servants extricate themselves from a muddle they so often neglect to drag their master and mistress out too."

"What success did you meet with?" asked the Sprightly Lady. "I'm longing to put a big gingham apron on and face the worst at once."

"I found that I was deplorably ignorant. I shall never forget my first morning's work. I arose at six, intending to have breakfast at half-past seven. It was a very cold day, and I suffered as I worked over the fire (which I ought to have made ready to light the night before, but had not), and as I was sweeping the walks and galleries I decided that a servant's life was neither easy nor pleasant. I hope I shall never outlive the feeling of sympathy for that class of women, which grew out of my aching hands and feet that morning. Armed with the boldness of ignorance, I undertook quite a little breakfast, — oatmeal, coffee, scrambled eggs, stewed potatoes, and muffins. Poor Maggie stood by at first, begging for just enough work to keep her warm, so I set her to scouring tins. Half-past seven came, — eight, — no breakfast. Maggie smiled in a respectful but superior manner. 'Never mind, Maggie,' I said, — for she was a girl with whom I could indulge my love for a little jest, with no fear of her taking advantage of me, — 'it was half-past eight I said this morning.' 'I think it was, mum,' she responded with Irish brevity. It was nearly nine when at last we sat down to breakfast; but fortunately everything was nice enough to satisfy our keen appetites. I kept up this toil, in an intermittent fashion, for several weeks. Generally, I worked all the morning and then went to bed for the afternoon, for I was not over strong, and being quite unused to such labor I wearied readily. Once Maggie ventured to call my attention to the fact that I found the work very hard; but I told her I was only a green girl. I asked her what she would think of me if I went to some lady and undertook her housework, and finding it very hard because of my greenness, told her she must pay me more than she would have to pay a competent girl, who could do it all quite readily; and Maggie had good sense enough to feel the force of this. I reminded her, too, that although she was at a training-school, she was receiving high wages. Usually, I said, a scholar pays the teacher; but in this school we have reversed matters, and the teacher pays the scholar. Throughout my work I was, although greatly fatigued, borne up by the consciousness that I was at last doing right. Indeed, I felt quite gay some of the time. I remember amusing Maggie much by remarking once, when I found I had made a blunder, that I'd dismiss that girl, for she didn't amount to anything.

"I merely mention this because I want to

call attention to the fact that in training servants it is far better to breathe a spirit of life into the work than one of discouragement, no matter if great cause for the latter may exist. You will find, I think, that servants will work better if, while plainly pointing out their errors, you also give them a hope of success.

"I was greatly aided in my kitchen work by Mrs. McNair Wright's excellent book, 'The Complete Home,' and I encouraged Maggie to read and put into practice some of its good suggestions."

"Do you really think, Mrs. Hughes, that we all ought to pass through such a course of training?" asked the Sprightly Lady, with a serious tone in her voice.

"I think it so earnestly that I wish it were possible for the State to establish training-schools, and to frame and enforce a law to the effect that no woman should marry until she could show a certificate of graduation from one of these; and I would it were possible for the State also to insist upon young men possessing certain qualifications before allowing them to marry."

"What, for instance?" asked the Sprightly Lady, with much animation. Indeed I thought, from their voices, that at this juncture all the ladies grew more interested and the speaker more interesting.

"We'll have to forego an answer to that, I fear, until we are called upon to discuss husbands."

"I only wanted to see if my Billy could have had me," said the Sprightly Lady.

"Don't you want to see if you could have had your Billy?" asked Dolly.

"I know I couldn't. I was only a poor, ignorant little society chit. I didn't know a dish-rag from a dish-pan."

"Why can't young men and women demand more of each other, without waiting for the law to aid them? There's nothing to hinder their taking matters into their own hands," said Dolly.

"Nothing but their falling in love," said Mrs. Hughes. "They need to have their interests protected until they become cool-headed enough to see clearly. Depend upon it, they will see sooner or later; and if they have been captivated by a pretty face, or the swing of a cane —"

"Poor Billy! he would have been counted out! That's what I married him for," murmured the Sprightly Lady.

"If they have nothing more substantial to rely on than that, sooner or later the romance will be dropped out of their union; and once dropped it is seldom picked up. It doesn't take a man very long to become disenchanted if there's nothing real to hold him."

"You speak of a man," said Dolly; "don't you think a woman becomes disenchanted too, if she finds her husband is not what she believed him to be?"

"I only spoke of a man because he is most apt to show it. I believe a woman feels this even more keenly, and I sometimes think she fathoms her husband's character more quickly than he does hers. But a woman is very reserved on these points; she generally keeps all this from the world; she often hides her discovery even from her husband."

Here I was seized with a terrible flutter. I wondered if Dolly had found me out and neglected to say anything about it. I determined to learn how much she knew, the moment the meeting was ended.

"I fear I must have become an old maid had the State acted upon Mrs. Hughes's suggestion," said the Imitation Millionnaire. "Kitchen work was always insufferable to me. I never undertook it."

Now, most of us knew, though she knew not that we knew, that her origin was humble, both as regards birth and worldly means, and that if she had never undertaken any form of domestic service she had simply shirked a clear duty.

"The work is not pleasant to any of us, I dare say," remarked Mrs. Hughes, quietly; "but I can assure the ladies that they would be most certain of escaping the frequent necessity of doing it, by knowing how. In other words, I believe that such knowledge on the part of mistresses would create a better class of servants, and we should cease to suffer from this frequent changing."

"I believe that is true, Mrs. Hughes," said Dolly. "I have found that the more I learn about housework, the stronger hold I have on my servants. I have found that I can generally do better with my nurse than with my other servant, and I believe that's because I know about every part of her work."

"I don't agree with you," said the Imitation Millionnaire; "I think servants respect a mistress more if she does not pretend to compete with them in their department. I always say to my cook, if she asks how to make a dish, 'That is your business, not mine.'"

"One of the very best housekeepers I ever saw," said the Sprightly Lady, "knew nothing of practical housework."

"Oh, Jenny," exclaimed Dolly, "that's hardly a fair instance! I know whom you mean; but she lives in New York, and is rich, and has a wonderful faculty for controlling those beneath her."

"I don't think we should find it safe to take such an one as a criterion, though many do," said Mrs. Hughes. "All over our land we hear this cry about worthless servants. I believe it is safe to assert that the United States takes the lead for the household ignorance of its women, both mistresses and maids. I know, by the servants who have come to me, something of the style of mistresses in this city. Before I learned housework thoroughly myself I changed often, and so had an opportunity to judge. I received excellent recommendations from ladies for very incompetent girls. I remember one Irish cook who had been paid high wages. She could take hold of a dinner-party and manage that fairly well. Her cake, pies, and desserts were generally good, but her cooking was all of the richest. She thought that, to excel, her dishes must swim in butter, coffee must be black, and so on. She had no idea how to make simple vegetables delicious, — potatoes white and foamy; rice with every kernel soft, white, and distinct. Through the surprise or displeasure of my servants when they saw how I superintended matters, I have learned how rare it is for mistresses to keep accounts, to watch their grocery and butcher bills, and the larder, that nothing be wasted. Of course these spoiled servants resent being watched; but what do the men of the family think of this free-and-easy housekeeping? I always dislike to mention husbands in this way, because there ought to be no distinct opinion or interest in this matter. Husband and wife should be one here, certainly. I assure you that many a man is driven to discouragement — worse still, is pressed into dishonor — by the waste of his household. He may not see this, but he feels the effect of it sooner or later. I am far from saying that every man who fails does so because of some woman's extravagance, for I believe that in his way a man is as often extravagant as his wife; but I do say this: lack of knowledge on the mistress's part necessarily means waste. It is her duty to save, and set her husband an example of thrift. I place women very high. I look to them to save the men, — first by performing their own duty, and next by influencing their husbands to do likewise."

Here Mrs. Hughes suddenly paused, and said she feared she had taken too much time for one afternoon, and that she would say no more that day.

Dolly assured her that they felt grateful for her words, and that the time had seemed short to them. I was glad to hear the other ladies heartily join with Dolly in this. Even the Imitation Millionnaire allowed there might be something which it would be proper to learn, and if so, she would be happy to know of it.

The Pale Lady was the most quiet; but Dolly assured me that she seemed interested — really animated for her, which meant, probably, that she had smiled faintly once.

CHAPTER IV.

SELECTING AND MANAGING SERVANTS.

"OH, Griff! you outrageous creature! What have you done!" exclaimed Dolly, as by means of a covert glance over my shoulder she caught the heading of my articles. "I said we would n't be a club! And then such a wretched name! You ought to be ashamed of yourself!"

"Can't help it, Dolly. You said you would n't vote, and you voted; you said you would n't club, and you clubbed; and as you talk about Biddies, why, the Biddy Club you must be. It can't be helped, my dear. It is one of those things which, growing out of circumstances beyond one's control, become the inevitable."

Dolly was not wholly satisfied; she was about to say that she would n't speak to me for a week, when suddenly the remembrance of her spring bonnet, for which I was to call the next day, and of her jacket dated the day after — not to mention Ray's first tooth, which was being set in an enamel breastpin at the jeweller's — came to her mind, and she caught her breath just in time.

The Club assembled that afternoon, and were about to open the discussion, when the Sprightly Lady exclaimed, —

"We let you off too soon last time, Mrs. Hughes, for you did n't tell us what became of Maggie. I 've lain awake nights wondering if she adhered to you."

Mrs. Hughes laughed and said, —

"Perhaps that story were better left untold. About two weeks after opening my private training-school, I wrote a friend that I had learned much and had saved my servant. The first proved true; but I was obliged, somewhat later, to add a postscript to my letter, for I lost Maggie."

"She wearied of well-doing, poor sinner!" sighed the Sprightly Lady.

"Yes, at last. I think that if I had been a competent housewife when I engaged her, I might have made an excellent servant of her; but it was very hard for her to alter her entire mode of work for a mistress who was only a learner herself. To a certain extent the girl was being experimented upon, and in a vague way she felt this. All ended pleasantly between us. She wished to live nearer her Catholic Church, and made that the excuse for leaving.

But so far from regretting my new course, I pursued it even more systematically and steadily, and learned little by little—"

"You don't mean to say you continued doing all your work!" exclaimed the Imitation Millionnaire.

"No, I never did it all, and at the end of two weeks I ceased doing as much as I had done; but I was in and about the kitchen a certain time each day, and I kept learning more and more about my work. For one thing, I found that if I were doing it, I should need many little conveniences and appliances which the kitchen then lacked, and these I supplied as I was able."

"I've given that up," said the Imitation One, with a resigned sigh; "they won't use such things when they have them."

"I compelled their use until the girls found they could n't well do without them. We must never lose sight of the fact that if we do our whole duty by our servants, we shall educate them."

"Oh, I've made an end of that!" said the Millionnaire. "I've done with missionary work."

"So many of us feel at times, I dare say," said Mrs. Hughes, with that clear-cut courtesy which was peculiar to her when she wished to administer a polite rebuke; "but, unfortunately for our peace of conscience, God has not given up requiring such work of us."

The Millionnaire began to be troubled with a cough, and Mrs. Hughes proceeded: —

"I think, as I have finished Maggie now, some other one of the ladies had best do the talking."

"No, Mrs. Hughes," said the Sprightly One, "we want to hear from you."

"You have had the most experience, and it's but just you should do the most talking. We only ask the privilege of interrupting you when we have anything to say," observed Dolly.

"Yes, we reserve the privilege of all side remarks," said one who had spoken but seldom.

"Supposing," said the Practical Person, "we were all of us proficient housewives, what would you advise as the first step in the regulation of our service?"

"There is an adage which I can recall but feebly, but it's something to the effect that one must catch a bird before he eats it. The first step in this servant question is to choose wisely. I look back now upon the time when I was changing every week or so, and I can see how little shrewdness I showed in the matter of my choice. If a girl comes to you all dressed in cheap and gaudy finery, you don't want her. Even if she's dressed soberly, but with clothes beyond her means and station, — imitation seal-skin cloak, kid gloves, or anything of that kind, — you don't, as a general thing, want her."

"Oh, I never trouble myself about their dress, so they do their work and look well," said the Imitation Millionnaire.

"I don't think that's any of our business," remarked one of the Silent Members.

"I do," said Dolly; "but I don't know just what to do about it. I'm often bothered by having my cook put more white skirts into the wash than I do, and I've known her to spend a long time ironing fancy lace collars."

"I hold that it is both our right and our duty to prevent this," said Mrs. Hughes. "To a certain extent, the large majority of servants are minors, — not in actual age perhaps, but in judgment, intellect, and reasoning capacity. They need to be controlled for their own good. By reason of our superior education and position, we ought to possess a great influence over them. I believe that God expects this, and holds us accountable for it. Many of our servants are foreigners; they come from countries where they received very small wages and dressed in homely, coarse, strong garments. Here they're paid much more, and before long they begin to ape ladies in their attire. They are not able to get the best, so they deal in the imitation, —

spending all their wages for even this. When they fall ill they often have to depend on their relatives for support, and in some cases these relatives are barely able to take care of themselves. One girl out-dresses another, and straightway a false spirit of emulation is aroused. Some servants lay up money, but my experience has led me to think that most of them spend all they earn; more than that, they are often in debt to some obliging friend, and instances are terribly common of girls who have been tempted to dishonesty and other crimes by their desire for dress."

"What can we do about it?" asked Dolly.

"Forbid it."

"But supposing most ladies allow it, then we should be unable to get servants."

"Yes, there is much danger of that," said Mrs. Hughes; "and, as I understand it, you wish to have clubs like this formed, so that ladies can be induced to make some uniform rules on these very subjects."

"Yes, that is it," said Dolly; "but it will be long before these clubs are universal, even if ours meets with success and starts others. And what is one to do in the mean time?"

"After I had trained myself and found out what I wanted from my servants, I used to reason in this way: if I am going to require some extras, I must offer some extras. I used to patronize two intelligence offices by turns, — both very good places, — and there I soon acquired a certain reputation as a mistress, so that before a girl came to apply for the place she knew about what to expect. I did not learn all this at the time, but I was told afterward that I was spoken of at these places as very strict, very particular; but girls were assured that I would treat them with the greatest kindness and the greatest justice, and that with me they could have some privileges not granted by most mistresses."

"What, for instance?" asked the Sprightly Member.

"That of time, principally. Sundays my cook and nurse alternated. One morning the cook went to church; that afternoon she took care of the children, and the nurse went out right after our two-o'clock dinner and stayed till bedtime. At about half-past six the cook was also free to go. The next Sunday the cook had the extra time; and so on. During the week the cook could go out one day right after our dinner, which we took at two, and stay till bedtime, — the nurse washing the dinner-dishes and getting tea; another day the nurse had that privilege, and the cook attended to her duties. Besides this, each girl had one evening, being free to go at seven and to leave the rest of her work for the other servant. Washing and ironing days the nurse cooked and cleared away the breakfast. My washings were heavy; but with this help, the girl, by rising early, could end her work in the afternoon and rest one or two hours before tea. My ironing was all done in a day. For some years, now, we have washed on Monday and ironed Wednesday."

"Why do you prefer that arrangement?" asked the Millionnaire.

"The suggestion came to me from a servant, who asked permission to wash Saturday, so that she could have a day of comparative rest before ironing. Washing and ironing are the hardest work the girls have; and I think it is better, for the health's sake, if we can separate them. It was no trouble to me to do so. Indeed, it was a convenience in the winter, for the clothes rarely dried in one day. In summer the girl packed the wash into two large baskets, covered them over, and set them aside until late Tuesday afternoon, when she sprinkled and folded them."

"If you had had dinner at night, Mrs. Hughes," said the Practical Person, "you could not have given your servants so much time."

"We did dine at night, until Mr. Hughes wished to change the dinner-hour on the score of health; and I think my servants had fully as much time, only, of course, it was taken differently. I let them go in the forenoon and stay until about four in the afternoon."

"Mrs. Hughes," said Dolly, "will you please give us a plan of your work?"

"Certainly; but it may not suit your households. Monday we washed; Tuesday, swept the upper part of the house and baked; Wednesday, ironed; Thursday, the silver was cleaned, and the upstairs windows, and then, at about three, the cook generally went out. I never had an inflexible time for this, but I thought it would be pleasanter for her to know beforehand when she could go, so as to arrange to meet friends, and generally this was her day. Friday morning she swept downstairs, and after dinner sewed and took care of the children for the nurse, who usually went out that day."

"Well, if your cook would sew, it was remarkable. Mine will never do an extra thing," said the Millionnaire.

"My cook is perfectly willing to sew, but it is I who object, for I don't admire her style," said the Sprightly Lady.

"I generally selected some of the simplest mending for her afternoon's work, — the clothes that needed buttons, or some of the oldest garments that were not worthy of fine work. I have had cooks who sewed quite well, but that was not usual. Saturday, the baking, scrubbing, and downstairs windows filled the day. Our baking was very light, or we could not have accomplished so much; but we had several ends in mind, and tried to compass them. First of all, I wanted on Saturday to have some little dessert made for Sunday. We also had beans baked; for both my husband and myself were fond of them, and as they are nutritious we made an entire dinner off them every wash-day, with, of course, the accompaniment of bread and butter, some pickles, perhaps, or sauce. If I wished to have for Sunday any meat that would require long cooking, this was at least partially done on Saturday. On Tuesday we always had something prepared for the ironing-day dinner, and on both Tuesday and Saturday some tea dishes, such as veal loaf, jellied chicken, sauces, and so on. These we would use for tea on wash-day and ironing-day, or when either servant was out; so that at those times, with bread and butter or toast, or rolls (which were made with the bread), we had a nice tea ready without any effort."

"Did n't you bake cake or pies?" asked a Silent Member.

"Sometimes, but not often; we generally had some nice fruit-cake on hand. Two or three loaves of this would, in a cake-box, keep until it was eaten, — several months, perhaps. We did n't care for it when we were alone; but if some friends dropped in we could have a few slices on the table, to be taken or not as one chose. We used to laugh about this, and say we thought such cake injurious for ourselves, and so we kept it for guests. Some weeks we had thin crisp cookies made, but it was generally so long before I could get them eaten that I did not have them often."

"Your children must have been wonderful!" said the Imitation Millionnaire.

"My children were seldom allowed to taste even the plainest cake. I think many people make a great mistake in this matter. Growing children need very plain, nutritious, nicely-cooked food. It would be better for all of us to eat such, but they especially, with their bones and muscles forming, need that and no other. Now, time is saved, and money is saved (in the health gained), by providing such food, and omitting the great quantity of cakes and pies that is consumed by almost every average-sized American family. It has been my effort for years to simplify my work as much as possible."

"Did n't you care for your table?" asked the Sprightly One. She had quite a knack for table arrangements.

"My table was my pride," said Mrs. Hughes, with a quiet smile.

"Oh, we've all heard of Mrs. Hughes's table," said the Millionnaire, politely. But I fancied I could detect a sort of undercurrent of surprise that the table should have established such a reputation, in view of recent revelations.

"How did you manage, Mrs. Hughes, to have your table at once so simple and so elegant?" asked Dolly.

"I contrived early in my housekeeping experience to buy very pretty dishes. I bought them with money I saved by denying myself knick-knacks. My set was white china, very thin and nice; and besides this, I gathered, piece by piece, quite an assortment of dainty extra dishes."

"And did those satisfy hunger?" exclaimed the Sprightly One. "What a model Mr. Hughes must have been! I can fancy Billy's rage if I were to try to lunch him on an exquisite cracker-dish."

Everybody laughed at this, but Dolly exclaimed, —

"Now, Jenny! you know you said, only the other day, that your handsome little dishes had many a time kept guests from seeing that you had n't much for lunch!"

"I didn't say they'd fooled Billy, though! He looks right through them to what's inside."

"It sounds absurd, perhaps," said Mrs. Hughes, "but it is nevertheless true, that delicious cooking and handsome serving make very simple dishes appetizing. Now, a frequent breakfast with us — for we had it Sundays, and washing and ironing days — was fruit, oatmeal, and eggs. If I had had those all on the table at once, and in common ware, they wouldn't have amounted to much; but I had a lovely odd dish for the fruit, another for the oatmeal, and still another for the eggs (the latter being accompanied by dainty little egg-cups), and each one of these articles of food formed a separate course."

"What, each egg!" whispered the Sprightly Person.

"Perhaps you have seen Mrs. Henderson's cook-book. She strongly urges the course system. She says if you have but two dishes, you will find that if you serve them in two separate courses they will go farther, and your table will be more elegant."

"It's all very well to talk of thin china and glasses and unique dishes," said the Practical Lady; "but I should say we'd either got to have a different class of servants, or wash all these things ourselves."

"I don't quite agree with you," said Mrs.

Hughes. "I suffered more or less damage at first, but then I made some changes that effected much good. I bought an extra table; it was only a common one, but I placed it in the dining-room close to the kitchen door. When we were not eating I kept a pretty cover on it, and a few books and papers; but at meal-times the servant laid these aside and cleared the dishes on to it. I made a rule that no silver, china, or fancy dish was ever to be taken out into the kitchen, excepting as was necessary to serve a meal. Then I made another rule, to the effect that I should hold my cook responsible for anything broken. I told her I counted a dish broken if it was even slightly nicked. I looked over the dishes with her every little while, and if there was any nicked piece I took it out and she had to replace it."

"Supposing she couldn't find another such dish," said Dolly.

"My china was easily matched, being white; as for the odd pieces, occasionally she would be unable to duplicate one of these; in that case she had to forfeit as much of her wages as I thought right. I was forced to make this rule to protect myself, as I had so much broken. Mr. Hughes thought it rather hard; but I told him it made a more careful woman of my servant, and so was a benefit to her, and it saved me from suffering from another's carelessness."

"Did you have your nice dishes washed in the dining-room?" asked the Millionnaire.

"Yes, right on my smaller table; and I told the girl she could be longer at that work than she was washing the kitchen dishes, and so be more careful. Of course, I used my judgment in the matter of replacing. If a girl lived with me a long time without breaking anything, I would sometimes excuse an accident of this kind. Then, again, once in a while the circumstances were such that the fault was in itself excusable; but generally I enforced the rule, and I found that breakages diminished with pleasing rapidity. Under some circumstances, after finding it necessary for a servant to replace a dish, I have made a present of the money to her later. As the nurse often washed the dishes, of course she was once in a while at fault; but I trusted to her honor to make good any carelessness. I had to select one of the girls and hold her responsible, but I felt sure the nurse would not let the cook suffer unjustly."

"You had great confidence in their truthfulness," said the Millionnaire, with a superior smile.

"Yes, and with great cause. I have had much experience with these girls, and I can say now that after I had passed my first housekeeping year and learned how to choose servants, I never had but one who was untruthful. That was an Irish cook; and even she would tell the truth if I pinned her down to it, but otherwise she would evade me at times."

"I wish you would teach us how to choose so marvellously well," sighed the Sprightly Lady.

"All there is about it is to select a quiet, steady-looking, willing girl. You want her to be intelligent, for unless she is she will not make a good servant; you cannot reason with her, and she can never advance in learning. I always preferred such a girl, with medium acquirements, to one who knew more and thought she knew all."

"I don't believe one girl out of a hundred would stand it if I made such rules about dishes," said the Practical Person.

"I had a great many servants, and although some of them demurred a little, none of them seriously objected, and when they left it was generally because I sent them away; for I changed often in my efforts to find a girl who would do excellent work. I talked plainly with them, telling them that if I were to go into their room and break or damage something belonging to them, they would think it strange if I did not replace it, and I should feel very mean if I did not. I told them, too, that if I rented a furnished house, an inventory of the articles in that house would be handed me when I went in, and then I would be held accountable for everything. As for the natural wear and tear of utensils, I had nothing to say; but certainly it would be very unjust to let me suffer for any actual carelessness of theirs. Often the most difficult part was to convince a girl that she was at fault, especially when a dish or glass was only slightly nicked. She was not always conscious of having done this, and thought it might have happened at the table; but I always told her she could look at the dishes before she washed them, and if she found any such damage she must let me know, and that would relieve her of blame."

"What would families who are crowded with work do, Mrs. Hughes, if the cook stopped half an hour to look over the dishes after every meal?" asked the Practical Person.

"They can't carry matters so far, of course. If a woman has a large family and moderate means, she will be forced to put up with a great many things that can be arranged differently in smaller or wealthier households, for the same reason that she must dress more simply than richer women. But I do think that as far as actual breakages are concerned, we ladies might combine to require our servants to repair such damage. This is another point which we ought to gain by holding council on the subject, as we are doing to-day."

"Mrs. Hughes," said one of the more Silent Members, "you spoke awhile ago of a servant's dress. Did you make any special rules about that?"

"Not until I had been much annoyed by their poor dressing. They were either under-dressed or over-dressed half the time, so I finally adopted a uniform for them. It consisted of a calico gown made with full skirt and plain waist. Each girl had three of these suits, and wore one mornings with gingham aprons, and another afternoons with white aprons, white surplice, or collar, and cap. Every week the morning gown of the preceding week was put into the wash and the afternoon gown took its place, while a fresh one was worn in the afternoon."

"Could you get your girls to wear caps? I have had some trouble about that," said the Millionnaire.

"Some girls did not object at all; others did, and at first I did not insist upon it. But Mr. Hughes and I were both so annoyed by finding an occasional misplaced hair, that I made a rule that the cook must wear a close cap whenever she was on duty. I told her no man would think of cooking without one; all bakers wore them, and she must. The nurse's cap was different, and was worn because it helped keep the hair tidy and made the girl look neat. As these caps were more or less becoming, few objected to wearing them; the chief trouble was about doing them up and keeping a clean one always on hand. I know that in some cities the girls have rebelled against these caps. I read some time ago that in England many of the servants had refused to wear them. But whatever we think best to do about the nurses and waitresses, I think we should insist upon our cooks wearing close caps when they are cooking. I did n't succeed in adopting this uniform until I was able to help the girls buy it; but I think we ladies could form a combination on this subject, as on others, and compel the wearing of some such simple, neat garb. Certainly it is cheap enough for them to afford it. I remember that when I visited one of the largest dry-goods stores in Montreal, I was struck by the fact that all the female clerks wore black gowns and white collars; and I was told that it was a rule of the house. I suppose the proprietors wished to do away with the tawdry styles so much in vogue among shop-girls. I have been told of some very select hotels and boarding-houses in this country where the servants are all required to dress in dark calicoes and white aprons."

"Do you object to a plain woollen gown?" asked Dolly.

"I do, because it absorbs perspiration and cannot be washed; and, worn by a working girl, it soon becomes unpleasant. I let them wear such gowns when they go out, if they wish."

"I suppose they dress as they please, then," said Dolly.

"Probably they burst forth in orange and red, to atone for their forced sobriety in the house," said the Sprightly Person.

"They might have done so, had they not been restrained."

"Did you make rules about that?" asked a Silent One.

"No, not exactly. You know there are many ways of restraining. You can bring a strong influence to bear upon a girl, and improve her taste."

"Yes," said a Quiet Lady; "I had an Irish cook who always wore a long white feather on her hat, and a gay gown, when she went out. I made her a present of a pretty, simple, gray suit, and talked to her kindly, until at last she came to dress quite modestly."

"That is certainly the best mode; but all girls are not amenable to such control. I had an Irish servant who, though lax about dress when doing her work, would go out of an evening wearing a brocaded velvet, with a button-hole bouquet, fancy hat, and so on. I believe the girl's character was good; but I told her that her foolish mode of dress laid her liable to very unjust and injurious suspicions. She did not mend her toilet, and for this and various faults I dismissed her."

"What do you think about our girls' wearing frizzes?" asked one of the Silent Members.

"To friz or not to friz, is now the question," said the Sprightly Young Person.

"I prefer to have them wear their hair plain; but then they are human. They wish to look well, and in cases where a little crimping will greatly increase their good looks I have never forbidden it. Sometimes we have compromised; they have worn plainly-dressed hair at home, and crimped hair when going out. Two things I have always emphatically forbidden: one, the wearing of bushy bangs, or a mass of frizzes, — frizzes so seldom combed that hairs are always falling from them; and another, appearing with the hair done up in any kind of crimping papers or pins. It is mortifying to think that there are so-called ladies who not only appear around their houses so, but even sit down at table with their hair done up in crimps."

"If a servant has no occasion to come into the dining-room, do you allow her to wear her hair so in the kitchen?" asked the Practical Person.

"By no means!" said Mrs. Hughes, with a somewhat heated emphasis. "I have always told them that if they wished to crimp their hair they must put it up at night and take it down in the morning."

"But in the summer the heat will take all the crimp out of hair in the course of a few hours," said the Practical Lady.

"Yes, so they have told me; and to prevent this I let them wear a little black lace veil, bound tightly over the hair after the papers are taken out. This does not look badly, and it preserves the crimps."

But just here Mrs. Hughes glanced at the clock, and rose abruptly.

"I do not want to leave you in exactly the same way as last time, but I must say that if I had not apologized then for keeping you so long, I should certainly do so now."

"Don't apologize, Mrs. Hughes," said Dolly; "'art is long,' and so are some servant girls, and we want to make the most of them."

"I should say some are long!" ejaculated the Sprightly Lady. "My last maid was seven feet, if she was an inch. She looked like a pair of mounted tongs. I respected her highly. I was really afraid to do anything else; and then, she seemed so beautifully adapted by Nature for the highest of everything."

CHAPTER V.

SOME DIFFICULT PROBLEMS.

AS soon as the ladies were all assembled, Dolly opened the meeting by saying, with some hesitancy, —

"Mrs. Hughes, I would like to ask you a question on a rather delicate and unpleasant subject."

"Oh, don't!" exclaimed the Sprightly Lady; "pray don't let's have anything delicate or unpleasant."

"We must," persisted Dolly, laughing, "for I crave information. 'I want to know,' as some Eastern people say. You spoke about the woollen gowns worn by servants becoming unpleasant from perspiration. I have had so much trouble with my servants on that account. Their room is always disagreeable to me, — and I have wondered if they bathe as often as they should."

The Millionnaire laughed.

"I can tell you in a word that they don't," said she.

"I have feared so," said Dolly; "but what can we do about it?"

"Do the best we can, and put their room as far off as possible," said the Imitation Millionnaire.

"If I may be allowed to differ, I would like to suggest another way," said Mrs. Hughes. "We can require our servants to bathe, and keep their rooms so that we may enter them without dread."

"But it's such a delicate subject to broach," said Dolly. "I could scarcely bring myself to tell a girl to take a bath. I should feel I was insulting her."

"As a general thing, you will find that those girls who need to be told are not very sensitive on the subject. I have had exceptions to this rule; but still I know of no other way for a lady to protect herself and her house from the consequences of a servant's personal neglect, than by requiring the girl to take proper care of herself. So long as we are upon this subject of bathing, I may as well say that there are others besides servants who neglect this part of their toilet."

"Oh, I know that!" exclaimed Dolly. "My physician once said that I would be amazed if he should tell me the difficulty he experienced in inducing those who claimed to be ladies to take care of their health in this respect."

"I don't think he need have spoken of ladies in particular," said Mrs. Hughes, "for I have heard physicians say that personal cleanliness was really very rare. There are many who think a weekly bath all-sufficient, and some take but a semi-monthly."

"Well, you know, Mrs. Hughes," said one of the Silent Members, "many people regard much bathing as injurious; even doctors disapprove of it sometimes."

"Yes, I know; they talk of bathing away the flesh, lowering the vitality, and so on. But I can never understand how they can recommend people to carry about, on their clothes and their persons, all that waste of the system which every intelligent man or woman knows the skin throws off daily if it does its lawful work."

"But don't you think there is such a thing as excessive bathing?" persisted one of the Silent Ladies.

"Certainly; but few of us fall into that error. I think that too frequent warm baths are weakening, and I know that some people are not able to take cold baths because they have not vitality enough to react. Still, I believe that is because they are not in a natural condition. But I have never yet seen any one in reasonable health who would not feel benefited by a quick sponge — not plunge — bath taken daily, with, if needful, just the chill off the water. For many people, doctors recommend a little rock or sea salt dissolved in the bath water. This sponging, with a semi-weekly thorough warm bath, will answer all the needs of cleanliness."

"I have been told," said Dolly, "that it is better to use the hand in a bath than a sponge or cloth. What do you think, Mrs. Hughes?"

"The only advantage of a sponge is, that in a quick bath it more readily and neatly gathers up the water than the hand can; but I don't doubt that an after rubbing with the latter is excellent for strengthening purposes. Some doctors are very much opposed to the use of a sponge, because it is so liable to retain impurities."

"Did you require your servants to bathe every day?" asked the Practical Person.

"No; but they were always obliged to bathe twice a week, and if they chose to do more I was of course pleased. Another point which I was forced to emphasize with them was the wearing of different clothing at night from what they wore in the daytime; and here again it is not servants alone who are at fault, for I have known many so-called refined people who indulged in the really unclean practice of wearing the same underclothing night and day both. Some of my servants had to be told to wear nightgowns; but most of the more respectable girls had these, though all of them failed to have different flannels for night and day. I was especially strict with my nurse upon these points, for she brought a cot into the nursery, and slept there nights in order to watch over the children, and of course I wished her to be very tidy personally."

"I suppose, of course, you don't permit your servants to use the bath-room?" said the Millionnaire.

"Certainly not; they have a small bath-tub in their room, and separate bath-towels."

"I think, Mrs. Hughes," said the Practical Lady, "that one would have to occupy a very independent position in order to make all these requirements of servants."

"That is true; but I managed very early in my married experience to place myself there, and I think others could do the same if they chose. Before I had kept house three years I made most of these conditions with my maids, and before four years I made them all."

"You must have been richer than some of the rest of us. I know money gives independence," said the Practical One, with a sigh.

"No, I think not; for my husband and I began our married life with modest means, and it was many years before we were even what would be called well off, financially. But we were of one mind upon this servant question, both being agreed to have servants, — good servants too. The latter we knew would cost money, but we regarded them as less expensive in the end, saving us, as we felt sure they would, much of the wear and tear of life. But in order to obtain such service, we were obliged to deny ourselves many things. We made our choice between handsome furniture, handsome clothing, and entertainments, on the one hand, and good servants on the other. That is to say, our house was furnished simply, — indeed, much of the furniture was home-made; but we used to think it was the loveliest house we ever saw, for it had so many simple but pretty decorations; then we dressed in good taste, I hope, but very plainly, and we went to the theatre or opera only as a great and unusual treat. When we first kept house we had one servant; but as soon as a little child came to our fireside we kept two."

"Then you believe in nurses, Mrs. Hughes?" said one of the Silent Members.

"Yes, most decidedly."

"Oh, Mrs. Hughes!" exclaimed the Sprightly Lady. "I fear, then, you are opposed to the devoted-mother theory!"

It was seldom that the Sprightly Lady's fun

ever hurt any one, and Mrs. Hughes in particular understood her so well, and thought so much of her, that she was not likely to be wounded by these little pleasantries; but this time I saw a faint trace of pain cross her face. It quickly passed, and was followed by such a beautiful look — a look so brimful of motherhood — that she had no need to speak, nor did she try. Dolly, however, spoke with great spirit and energy: —

"There seems to be a popular fallacy abroad to the effect that the more jaded and faded a woman looks, the more motherly she must be; or, to put it in another form, that unless she is jaded and faded she can't be motherly."

"Does n't that fallacy, as you call it, spring from the fact that a mother's duties are such that if she performs them properly she must look more or less worn out?" said the Practical Person.

"I must disagree with you there," said Mrs. Hughes. "Before I had children of my own, I supposed that what you speak of was a necessary part of motherhood, and I dreaded it; for I prized my youth and fresh looks, and I knew my husband did also. But I thought then, as now, that no home could be complete without children. I was passionately fond of them, and I made up my mind to the sacrifice. But I very soon saw that I had been misled in that respect. I found that by the exercise of good common-sense and intelligence I could have my children begin life with health, and could, most of the time, preserve that health. I found that by feeding a baby properly, and training it to good habits, I could make it of very little trouble. As I have said, from the first I kept a nurse-girl, not alone for the care of the child, but because its coming greatly increased the family sewing. If I had undertaken to do all, I should have been constantly tired, besides finding no time to refresh my mind and body with reading and study."

"Did your nurse do the sewing?" asked the Practical Person.

"She did all the mending and almost all the plain sewing of the whole family; and I have even had some dressmaking done by her."

"She must have differed widely from my nurse. If I get her to do the mending I think I've achieved a victory. I have to hire my sewing," said the Millionnaire.

"I rarely ever hired a particle of sewing for the children, and very little for the rest of us," said Mrs. Hughes.

"But how could your girl accomplish it?" asked the Practical Person.

"She did it in the time that most people's nurses are holding or amusing the baby. My babies, from the first, were taught to amuse themselves."

"But didn't she take them outdoors?" asked a Silent Lady.

"Yes; but in the winter they did not remain long, and in the summer the nurse sat out in the yard, by the carriage or hammock, and sewed. When they were old enough to walk, they minded her voice, so she could easily sew, and at the same time give them all needful attention while they played with their toys or dug holes in the sand. My babies were all taught to sleep right through the night; by dint of a little management they were gradually trained to sleep late in the morning, and that gave the nurse about two hours before she had to attend to them. Then, during their daily nap she was again free, so with a machine she could accomplish much sewing."

"I have rarely had a nurse who was willing to sew," said the Imitation Millionnaire.

"I made that a part of my engagement with my nurse," said Mrs. Hughes.

"But what did you do if she didn't know how to sew?" asked the Practical Person.

"I taught her. I had to teach all who came to me, to a certain extent; for even those who thought they knew how could not sew well enough to suit me. Fortunately, my dear mother taught me the very ladylike accomplishment of nice needlework, and there was nothing of that kind I could not teach my nurses. Some were much slower to learn than others; if a girl disliked sewing, and showed no desire or aptitude for learning, I did not keep her. I had to train my nurses in many ways, — always in the art of waiting on the table, which was one of their duties. Indeed, I have had so few servants come to me with any knowledge of this latter art, that I have all but decided that people out here must reach for themselves at their tables."

"Mrs. Hughes," said the Practical Person, "do you think it is right for a woman to be leading a life of leisure while her husband is working hard?"

"By no means," answered Mrs. Hughes. "But if she carefully superintends her entire household, if she watches over her children and attends to her studies and social duties, she will have little, very little spare time; she will be leading a very pleasant, but a very busy, working life."

"But you speak of social duties and studies," said the Practical Person. "I have always thought those came in the list of extras, — especially the studies, — and were only to be pursued by people of more or less wealth and leisure."

"It is undoubtedly true that they do require a certain amount of both. There is a class who have absolutely no time for them without neglecting some more pressing duty; but the majority of people in the higher walks of life are not, or should not be, so situated. Most of them can, by proper management, so arrange their time as to pursue all the occupations of which we have been speaking."

"Still," persisted the Practical Person, "the majority of husbands, even in the class of which you speak, are working hard, and it does not seem right for their wives to spend much time in mere amusement."

"Do you call it mere amusement when a woman is cultivating and holding a proper position in society?" exclaimed Mrs. Hughes. "Do you call it mere amusement when she is educating herself? Can you forget that children will grow, that their demands will change and increase? Some day they will desire and need society. Can a mother who has kept no place in society furnish them with suitable companions? Companions of some kind they will have, you may be sure, and if the mother is not ready to supply them, they will help themselves, so to speak. Can a mother who has not trained her own mind carefully and rigorously, hope to train the minds of her children? I think that it is almost as unfortunate for children to have an uneducated mother, — one who is lacking in intelligence, — as one who is lacking in principle. The great mistake of a large number of men and women who advocate maternal devotion is, that they always think of children as infants. The limit of motherhood in their minds is the care of those children during a period when their wants are almost purely animal. It is then, I claim, that a mother may and should economize her strength and time, to fit herself to respond to the wants of her children when their brains — their souls — begin to cry aloud. Motherhood, if properly viewed, is most noble and elevating. By reason of some differences of occupation and nature, the father is not usually able to attend to these matters. The social position of the family, the companions of the children, and their education depend almost wholly upon the mother."

"Don't you think schools answer the needs of education?" asked a Silent Lady.

"Yes; for those who cannot find it at home."

"Don't you believe in sending children to school?" asked the Imitation Millionnaire.

"I can only say that I would have considered myself painfully deficient in motherhood had I sent a very young child to school. My children were educated at home until they were quite large, — young men and women you might call them; and even then the home education went on and formed an important factor in the mental training. I had assistants, I myself only teaching certain branches, for it would be narrowing to a mind to receive all its education from one person; but my children have only just begun to go out of the house to school or college."

"I am afraid you don't believe in our public schools," said a Silent Lady, anxiously.

"They are noble institutions, for they bestow education upon thousands who would otherwise grow up to be ignorant, incapable, even vicious citizens. But I consider them poor substitutes for the training of an educated, liberal-minded mother."

"But, Mrs. Hughes," said the Sprightly Lady, "many will tell you that in its rough-and-tumble life at school a child learns what it cannot learn at home."

"That is deplorably true. I do not wish to depreciate all of that training, but I certainly have tried to protect my children from most of it. I consider it a payment a child makes for its education; but I always preferred to have my little ones learn for a smaller price. I know that many cultivated people maintain that it is best, for boys especially, to see something of the world. I insist that the primal object of home is the shielding of both boys and girls from that very world until their characters have been at least somewhat strengthened and moulded, and their tastes trained. This applies to very young children; as they grow older, I believe in giving them glimpses of the world; but parents must use great judgment and care in this, and study the peculiar needs of the individual child. I do not believe in letting either a young man or a young woman step out into the world in total ignorance of it, but I would have their knowledge come gradually, and only in proportion as their characters and training warrant it; and certainly I believe that we cannot too carefully guard tender childhood. In this matter of woman's education there is another point to be made. I feel the mother has some mental duties and rights of her own, apart from her children. Hamerton, in his 'Intellectual Life,' claims that the influence of any individual is elevating and useful just in proportion to the care bestowed on his own character and mind. In the case of people blessed with children, those children generally become their strongest incentive; so I have been looking at the matter almost wholly from that standpoint. But we must not forget that this standpoint is not the only one. It would seem as if this were a violent digression from our discussion of servants; but it seemed to come about naturally, and to be the legitimate outgrowth of that question as to a woman's right to keep a nurse-girl."

I watched the Pale Lady's face carefully during this latter discussion, and for the first time since the Club was formed I detected a look of interest there. It was but slight; yet on that face its presence was so unusual that it was much more marked, much more significant, than a look of deeper interest would have been upon any other face there. What, I said to myself, if Dolly's Club were the means of awakening this unhappy woman, of calling her to life, as it were! I speculated much as to the possible effect of the genuine awakening of such a character,— the effect upon her own life and that of her family. From her husband I anticipated little,— men of his age and stamp seldom change much for the better; but for the lady herself, and through her for her children, what might not be hoped if she really became interested in the subject of true motherhood? I thought of the young and growing characters depending upon this very woman for guidance and formation, and I saw that she could not be awakened to what was strong and good without affecting them powerfully. And as it all came before me, a respect which I had not felt before for Dolly's Club slowly crept into my mind, and I determined to apologize to my little woman for my previous levity.

"While we are upon the subject of nurses, Mrs. Hughes," said Dolly, "I would like to speak of an objection a lady once made to one of mine. She considered her too quiet, and was certain I'd have a stupid baby if I did n't employ a livelier nurse.

"There was, I should say, almost enough truth in the remark to blind one to its error. As a general thing, I think American children need quiet nurses. We are a nervous, excitable race, and everything which tends to check our natural tendencies in this direction is a help. On the other hand, it is undoubtedly true that little children left too much in charge of a very grave nurse would become unnaturally quiet, and possibly dull. But I should have no fear of this in a case like yours, where the little ones had a mother who did her duty. But, whatever may be said of small children, for babies, so far as I know, reputable physicians with one accord recommend soft tones, soft lights, and general quiet. This jolting of infants; this romping with and screaming at them, talking to them and teaching them, — this premature rousing of their little brains and weak nerves is by thoughtful people almost universally condemned. I know young mothers who hold the opinion that unless they talk to their babies the little ones will never talk for themselves. It's very well to begin to do some teaching in this respect when the child is old enough; but few parents wait for that time to come. Generally, this training begins at birth, — trying to make it laugh, and so on. All this noisy treatment of a baby is bad enough when indulged in by the members of the family, but when it comes from a noisy servant-girl I think it is unbearable. Aside from the injury to the child, the servant is allowed in this way to be entirely too familiar, and the mistress of such a maid will generally find that she will overstep the bounds of respectful conduct in other directions. I have always refused to keep a noisy servant."

"So have I," said Dolly. "I dismissed a very smart German nurse once for that reason alone."

There was a little further discussion and comparing of notes on this subject, and then the Club adjourned until the next week, — I making haste, upon my first opportunity, to see Dolly, and lay my increased respect and my contrition before her.

CHAPTER VI.

SCIENTIFIC HOUSEKEEPING.

"I HAVE been thinking much, since last seeing you, on the subject of scientific housekeeping," said Mrs. Hughes, when the ladies had reassembled once more.

"That is giving a new name to an old pursuit. It is something like making over an aged gown," said the Sprightly Lady.

"The name ought not to be new," answered Mrs. Hughes. "Indeed, I believe that no woman can ever be a fine housekeeper until she keeps house scientifically, — it matters not if she uses another word, so her methods are scientific. I often think of the government of the household in comparison with the government of the state or nation. We regard national government as a science worthy the studious attention of statesmen; we all look upon political economy as a science. Domestic government and domestic economy are, it seems to me, very similar in kind; for although, of course, they must be conducted on a much smaller scale, yet they involve many of the same principles. If women would only study their housekeeping in this light, I think the result would be a broadening of their minds as well as a great improvement in the housekeeping itself. The wife, the mother, is the chief executive; it becomes necessary to have servants under her, to carry out her orders, and she must choose wisely. I was lately reading of a recent President, that one of his distinguishing traits was his power to choose able officers and then take unto himself the credit of their work. This sounds rather unjust; but there is, nevertheless, a large admixture of justice in it. I never yet have seen valuable servants under an inefficient mistress. Such servants, trained in superior households, might possibly fall into the hands, so to speak, of an inferior mistress; but I feel confident that they would either shortly leave her or would degenerate. To a large extent a woman is justified in taking credit for the valuable service of her servants, for it is mainly due to her own efficiency. To begin with, she has chosen well, and this shows knowledge of character. She must possess much of the latter, or she will fail in governing her servants,—for she cannot successfully pursue exactly the same course with any two girls. I have had servants with whom I could have a few pleasant words, and even make an occasional jest, with no loss of my authority or dignity, and no possibility of their taking the slightest advantage of my treatment. I have had other servants who could scarcely receive a pleasant good-morning from me without straightway becoming familiar. The former class of girls are sometimes best governed by appealing to their sense of the humorous; with the latter class a uniform dignity, gravity, almost a severity of speech and action was necessary. Some servants — Irish, for instance — are easily controlled by an appeal to their goodness of heart; others, merely by relying on their sense of right and wrong. But it would take too much time even to try to set forth the various methods, especially as each particular system involves many shades and varieties necessary to suit different girls of even similar characters. I only cite these instances, to prove that there is much opportunity for the study of human nature in dealing with our servants. I can only make a passing reference to children, because they do not properly enter our discussions; but we can all see how earnestly we should study their characters and capacities, and I think the control of servants involves similar principles. There are many other points upon which a woman should exercise scientific knowledge. One is in the ordering of her cooking. Hamerton, among other authors, discourses in a most interesting manner on the effect of a man's diet upon his particular calling. Here is a deep study for a woman. She should know the needs of the household, and regulate the style of table to these needs."

"I don't understand," said a Silent One.

"If she lives in a cold climate, and her husband's business obliges him to be out of doors much of the time, she should provide him with considerable fat and carbon in his food, to keep him warm. If his occupation is sedentary, if he uses his brains much more than his muscles, she should know that he will be unable to digest very fat food, and that he mainly needs that which supplies the most nutrition in the smallest and most easily digested quantities and forms. This is sufficient to serve as an illustration; there are many books published now by able writers on the science of diet, and even on scientific cooking; and if a woman wishes, she can from them learn the needs of infants, growing children, the demands of life in various climates, at different times of the year, and in different occupations, — in short, all connected with this subject which would tend to the preservation of the health, vigor, and happiness of her household. Let me whisper to you, young married ladies, that much of your husband's amiability and tractability depends upon the way you feed him. There is a world of wisdom in that little thing called 'How to Cook Husbands,' which is going the newspaper rounds."

"My gracious! how I have failed in my duty!" exclaimed the Sprightly Lady. "But I'll clap Billy into the stewpan the moment I get home, and serve him up with caper-sauce. I'll make the stew, and he'll furnish the capers."

"It's all very funny," laughed Mrs. Hughes, "but it's serious too, — very serious. I was thinking the other day, what a mercy it is that God sees not as we see, otherwise He would be in the same danger of mistaking tired nerves for irritability, and dyspepsia for ugly temper. We have all, in our reading, run across the grave truth that much of the intemperance in the land is the result of poor feeding."

"For pity's sake, Mrs. Hughes!" cried the Frivolous Lady, "don't make us believe that one shoulders such a terrible responsibility when she undertakes housekeeping, or we'll all rush to boarding."

"I never found that I could evade a duty by running from it. When I forsook my housekeeping and went to boarding, as I have already told you, my duty followed me, and continually stared me in the face. It is a terribly responsible thing to live; but I don't think it best, for that reason, for us all to rush to suicide."

"But we will! we really will, Mrs. Hughes!" said the Sprightly Lady. "You see we don't yet know that there's any responsibility involved in living; but the moment we find it out, we shall feel more depressed than the poor youth of Germany did over 'The Sorrows of Werther.'"

"I think the Sorrows of Some Housekeepers would make a still more pitiful volume, and might result even more disastrously," said Dolly.

"Let us see if they cannot be averted," replied Mrs. Hughes. "We were considering the subject of scientific housekeeping. It is a favorite topic of mine, for I am very fond of housekeeping conducted upon this plan. I think that instead of being narrowing, as are the poorer methods, it is a very broadening and elevating occupation. I spoke of the study of human nature, and the art of scientific cookery. There are other points to be thought of; and foremost upon the list stands economy. The attainment of the best results with the least possible expenditure is worthy of careful study, and can be accomplished only by such. Many women economize by setting shabby tables, dressing meanly, and furnishing their houses bleakly; there is no science in that. But when you see an appetizing table, a neatly, attractively-clothed family, and a prettily-furnished house, and learn that but comparatively little money is expended upon it all, you may be sure that what the mistress lacks in silver she more than makes up in brains. Whether she calls herself so or not, the woman who presides over that home is scientific."

"I wish, Mrs. Hughes, you would tell us something about a nice yet inexpensive table," said a Silent Lady.

"The cook-books have many recipes for dishes that are simple and still attractive."

"Oh, I think most of these recipes seem so impracticable to beginners!"

"Yes, they do," said Mrs. Hughes, "and indeed many of them really are impracticable; but with the light of a little experience one can sift out those that are really of value. I can perhaps give you a few hints, and it may be that I can even offer you a few new recipes. I read in the London 'Spectator,' not long ago, an article on the expenses of living, and chief among those named was the supply of meat demanded by the household. Now, of course this meat-bill will differ in size in different families. With us, although we had four grown people to provide for (counting our servants), it was always very small. We rarely ever had meat at breakfast; our first course was fruit of some kind, the next oatmeal, cracked wheat, or something similar, and the last course consisted of coffee and eggs, and potatoes in different forms, with either toast, muffins, biscuit, or plain bread; occasionally our third course was merely coffee and waffles, or nice batter-cakes eaten with maple syrup. For dinner, our first course was generally soup; the next was some kind of meat, potatoes, one other vegetable, and some sort of pickles, spiced fruit, or jelly. Then we often had a simple dessert. We usually dined at night, but there were seasons when, for some reason, our dinner-hour was one or two o'clock. During such seasons, for tea in summer we had fruit, some kind of bread, occasionally a salad, and cookies or some other plain cake. The winter teas were more difficult for me to plan, but they differed mainly in the meat. Oysters formed a very nice treat, but owing to their expense an occasional one. Then I sometimes had a remnant of beef, chopped finely, seasoned, and served on thin slices of toast; or a bit of mutton was cut in small thin slices, and stewed with a little gravy made from the water in which it had first been boiled, and seasoned with a few capers. Near the end of the 'Buckeye Cook-book' there is a recipe for a really nice dish called 'Mother's Hash;' it is quite far removed from that hash made so famous by boarding-house fare, and although not precisely the dish for tea, was one we relished on a cold winter night. That portion of the 'Buckeye Cook-book' called 'Fragments' contains many inexpensive yet appetizing recipes by means of which housekeepers could vary their bills of fare to great advantage. I mention the 'Buckeye' not only because it is so good, but also because it is one which young housekeepers are most apt to possess."

"You spoke of salads, Mrs. Hughes," said the Sprightly Lady. "We are very fond of those, and I wish you would please tell of some that are pretty and simple."

"I know a few that possibly you already have. They are similar in style, though different in taste. One is what I call 'Bird's-nest salad.' Boil hard seven eggs; when cold, cut each in halves, take out the yolks, mash these till perfectly smooth, add one and a half table-spoonfuls of either olive-oil or melted butter, one even teaspoonful of mustard, a quarter of a teaspoonful of salt, mixing each ingredient into the eggs thoroughly and separately; lastly, add enough vinegar to give a flavor, but still leave the dressing stiff enough to stand in place. Next, wash and carefully look over a head of lettuce, — I say carefully, for otherwise you will be likely to spoil your salad by the addition of those little green bugs; spread the lettuce-leaves over the salad platter, always putting the smallest leaves around the edge for trimming. I cut or tear the large leaves, and arrange so that each half-egg shall rest upon a separate bit of lettuce, and can be so put upon the plate at table. Take the emptied whites of the eggs and stand them on the leaves so they will look like little cups. Cut off their pointed ends so they can stand more securely. I never placed them in any particular form, but nestled them here and there among the lettuce-leaves. Finally, fill them full — heaping full — of the salad-dressing. The effect of the whole dish is very pretty. Another somewhat similar salad is made of medium-sized cold boiled potatoes. Place the lettuce on the platter as before, make the same dressing, but add more vinegar, so that it will be softer. Cut each potato in very thin slices; place eight or ten of these on each leaf of lettuce and cover with the dressing. Make a sort of wreath around the edge of the platter by putting the chopped whites of the eggs in the small lettuce-leaves. Cauliflower salad is also very nice and very pretty. Take a small, shapely cauliflower, and after soaking it, head downward, in salt water for about two hours, to draw out any bugs, boil it until tender; it must not be soft enough, though, to fall apart. Place it on a platter, the edge of which you trim with tiny lettuce-leaves. In the cracks of the cauliflower place here an olive, there a tiny leaf of lettuce, and also here and there a few tiny bits of beets, cut in pretty shapes; place a few of these last around the edge of the platter. Pour the salad-dressing over the whole. A very appetizing dish for lunch or tea, with bread and butter, is meat salad. Chop fine a bit of beef, all fat or gristle being taken out before chopping. Add to this, one quarter as much potato, half of a small onion, and considerable parsley chopped fine. Mix the whole with the salad-dressing. Trim the platter's edge with lettuce, or if that is out of season, celery-leaves, or even bleached turnip-tops. Mould the meat into a nice shape, and cover it with the finely-chopped whites of the eggs. A pretty addition is three or five parsley-leaves stuck into the salad so that they stand erect above the whites of the eggs. This recipe, with a trifling difference, is one I took from Mrs. Wright's 'Perfect Home.' Tomato salad is very nice and pretty. Take medium-sized tomatoes, hollow them out, and fill with salad-dressing. Cover the tops with chopped whites of the eggs, and trim the edge of platter as you wish."

"Do you use the same dressing for all salads?" asked the Imitation Millionnaire.

"Yes, because we prefer it; but others might prefer another. A nice dressing is made of raw yolks beaten up with olive-oil, — a little of the latter being added at a time until the eggs become very stiff; then the mustard and salt are added, and finally the whole is made as thin as desired by the addition of vinegar. When one is in haste, the beating can be done with an egg-beater. This dressing is more expensive, as it requires considerable olive-oil. I prefer the other; and aside from the taste, an advantage to that is, that the whites of the eggs are all ready to use in various ways."

"We like a great deal of olive-oil; we are very fond of rich food," said the Millionnaire.

"Celery will make a nice salad, Mrs. Hughes," said the Sprightly Lady; "and it's easy to prepare. You just cut the nice part into short pieces, put these in the centre of the platter, pour the dressing over them, and trim the dish as you like. I should think that some finely chopped whites of eggs would be pretty to dress the top of this salad."

"Now we are on the subject of pretty dishes," said Dolly, "I must tell you of one I saw lately at a little evening company. The pulp of some oranges had been taken out, and the skins were filled with wine jelly, and on top of it all was some whipped cream. It was a beautiful and delicious dish."

"What became of the orange pulp?" asked the Practical Person.

"Why, that could always be utilized," said Dolly. "I didn't inquire, but I noticed that we had orange-cake that same evening."

"How interesting and instructive are the results of an observant mind!" said the Sprightly Lady.

"Mrs. Hughes," said a Silent One, "you spoke of doing with but little meat, and yet you seem to have had it as often as most people."

"We ate but little, so a roast of beef or leg of mutton of four or five pounds would last us several meals. In a measure, we made up in milk what we lacked in meat."

"So do we," said Dolly. "Our milk-bill is double our meat-bill."

"I should think you ought to keep a cow," said the Sprightly Lady.

"So we ought," answered Dolly, glancing furtively around toward the library where sat the scribe. Then she lowered her voice, but without avail, for my ear was trained on that subject, and could detect the most distant whisper in which the word "cow" was mentioned.

"My husband," murmured Dolly, softly, "doesn't like cows very much. He has had some trying experiences, but I hope that some day we'll keep one; it would really be economy for us."

"Never!" quoth I, in my retreat. I was quite firm on that point; for after having been frequently hooked, pushed, pulled, drawn, and all but quartered by a cow, I naturally evaded the species. In an unhappy moment, Dolly's father once made her a present of a cow; but after I had led a truly wretched life for several months, I told Dolly she must look out for another milkman; and later I told the cow that, rude as it seemed to disturb her dreams of permanency, she must seek another home.

CHAPTER VII.

MONEY MATTERS.

"MRS. HUGHES," said the Frivolous Young Lady, at the opening of the next Club meeting, "are you a supporter of Woman's Rights?"

"Oh, no," said Mrs. Hughes, "I am ardently in favor of Woman's Wrongs."

"Oh, Mrs. Hughes, you catch things up so quickly that one is fairly frightened!"

"If one could only be terrified into silence!" I thought, in secret.

"Of course, I mean strong-mindedness, Mrs. Hughes; I don't like to think it, but it really seems so. I don't believe my husband would be willing to have me come here if he knew that. I know he'd leave me if I thought as you do. He can't endure anything like strong-mindedness in a woman."

I made a mental note at this point to the effect that he certainly could find no fault with her. She was weak-minded enough to satisfy the smallest of men.

"Now that we have touched upon this question," said Mrs. Hughes, "I would like to say that it is lamentable that women in general are so ignorant of their rights."

She spoke in that womanly way of hers, so full of dignity and sweetness and so void of any frivolity or irritation. It seemed to me as if, in the face of such strength and womanhood, the Frivolous Little Person ought to have shrunk away beyond all possibility of recognition. I have had my laugh and my sneer too, perhaps, at Woman's Rights, when it has been voiced by some noisy, half-educated woman; but before such an one as Mrs. Hughes I can only doff my hat and listen. Unfortunately, the Frivolous Person showed no inclination either to remove her hat or to pay attention.

"Would you vote? Oh, Mrs. Hughes!" she exclaimed; and then added with polite afterthought, "Oh, well, of course I've no objection if a woman really wishes to wear pants and go to the polls; but it's queer taste."

"There are various branches of Woman's Rights," replied Mrs. Hughes, with quiet courtesy. "The one that has been especially in my mind of late is the financial. I do most earnestly wish women understood their rights in money matters. It would seem as if a discussion of this subject were alien to our purpose in meeting, but I cannot see how any woman can occupy her true position as mistress in her household, or regulate it properly, unless she bear her legitimate relation to the family purse. Many of the opposers of woman's voting are loud in lauding her position as queen of the domestic hearth. But the truth is, that very few women are queens; most of them are paid dependents, and poorly paid at that. Not long ago I heard a wife and mother say, in a moment of bitterness, that housekeeping was a very poor paying business; there was but little money in it, and less appreciation, and she thought women had better engage in something else. I have again and again had women say to me, with regard to the income received from my painting, that they envied me, they so wished they had some way of earning money of their own. Now, if they had wished for some way of increasing the family income, I could understand their feeling; but I cannot understand why a woman should regard what is earned at the office or store as belonging entirely to her husband."

"I think she feels so, Mrs. Hughes," said a Silent Member, "because her husband does. I believe most men have that feeling."

"I don't doubt it; and this opinion on the part of the husband must influence the wife.

It is natural that, under such circumstances, she should feel more or less unhappy over money affairs; but such an error should not really deceive her."

"But what can a woman do about it?" asked the Practical Person.

"There is a great deal to be done. In the first place, as with many other vexatious questions, the best time for settlement is before marriage."

"Oh, Mrs. Hughes! you believe in forcing a man to make a marriage settlement!" exclaimed Mrs. Frivolity.

"Yes, I believe in a written agreement of some kind. I also believe that before marriage one should understand a man's character as thoroughly as possible, and feel sure that he will not be unfaithful in any way, or try to defraud his wife of any rights. All important questions should be earnestly talked over before marriage, and the temper of both parties upon the various subjects learned. If harmony does not exist before marriage you may be pretty certain it will never come after marriage; and in such a case, for the happiness of both man and woman, the engagement ought to be ended. They really have no right to marry without harmony."

"That's all very well, Mrs. Hughes," said the

Sprightly Lady, "but two or three women in this world are already wedded. Must they forever despair of pin-money?"

"I hope not," said Mrs. Hughes. "If a woman has been so careless of her own and her husband's future as to marry without talking all these matters over and coming to a definite understanding, the next best thing for her is to have a post-nuptial conversation. She talks at a great disadvantage then, and unless her husband possesses rare qualities of manhood she will be made to feel this disadvantage. But I believe that a man must be extremely small who will not, sooner or later, see the truth that lies in this matter, if his wife presents it to him properly. I would not for the world have her complain or whine or scold about it; but she should, I think, in a quiet, womanly way, show him the injustice he is doing her in compelling her to ask him, from day to day, for fifty cents or a dollar or two, and show him how this latter course humiliates her. Let her tell him that when she married she understood that she and he were to form a firm in which each was equal partner. The old marriage service says, 'With all my worldly goods I thee endow;' few women ask for more than half. Some men claim that in any ordinary partnership both partners do equal work; but that is not quite true. I have known of many partnerships in which the actual physical and even mental labor was very unequally divided, although the division of the income had to be exact. One partner perhaps possessed an amount of influence which was thought to compensate for his lack of actual work, and so on.

"Now, there is no sum large enough to hire any one to fulfil the duties of a true wife, much less those of a true mother. I care not how many servants a woman may keep, or how comparatively easy her life may seem, the actual physical labor is the least part of it, — that can be hired, and without very great expense; but the love, the tenderness, the solicitude, the watchfulness, the brain-work, the companionship, the education, — all that goes to make up true wifehood, true motherhood, — no money on earth can hire. Now, does it not stand to reason that in simple justice all this should have a pecuniary value, as well as a value which money is not sufficient to recognize properly? Let a woman, then, with the dignity which grows out of conscious right, claim her half of the family income. A man may deny this claim, but in such a case the wife should, I think, assert her right, and tell him that this right remains, even though he refuse to recognize it; tell him that he may withhold her just share, as he might possibly succeed in evading the law and withholding the property of a ward, but that by so doing he is committing a great fraud, a sin against his wife and himself. It is a disgrace to our land of freedom and justice, that the law has not already taken this matter in hand. The money power is one which men of contemptible character, and also those of better character, in small and unworthy mood, hold over their wives; and since their manhood is not sufficient, the law should restrain them. The law recognizes a woman's right in the property if her husband attempts to sell it; and I hope to live to see the day when it will also recognize her right to the income from this property, and also from the office or store. A short time ago I took up an old magazine and read an article in which Dr. Holland discoursed very beautifully upon the sweetness of that ownership of the woman by the man in marriage. There is much sentiment in such a theory, much tenderness; but that should not blind us to the fact that it is none the less a relic of the barbarism that governed the relationship of man and woman ages ago, and that it has been the cause of great injustice and consequent unhappiness."

"Don't you think, Mrs. Hughes," said a Silent Member, "that men would give more to their wives if they had it? It seems to me that most of them are inclined to be very generous when they are able."

"I don't deny that, but I object to that word 'giving.' The money should be handed the wife as her right, her property, not as a gift. This would remove the sense of obligation under which so many men really expect their wives to live, for so-called generosity on their husband's part."

"I don't think my husband ever really saw this matter in its true light," said another of the Silent Members, "until two years ago. At that time he formed a partnership with an elderly gentleman who, because of his superior years, experience, and ability in that direction, took into his charge the financial branch of the business. In consequence of this arrangement, to which my husband had given his consent, he was forced to ask his partner for whatever money he wished to draw; and he grew more and more irritated and nettled under this condition of affairs, until finally he said he could stand it no longer, and had it changed. I did not fail to draw his attention to the analogy which existed between his position at the office and my position at home. I told him that although men supposed that women were made of something besides flesh and blood like themselves, and were not wearied or rendered nervous by crying children, or nettled and humiliated by monetary dependence, yet the reverse was the case. There were many minor circumstances attending that partnership which greatly benefited me at home, by presenting my cause in a more vivid light than I could otherwise have done. For instance, my husband would tell me of certain improvements he had effected at the office in the service there, or perhaps the furnishing, and say how opposed his partner was upon first mention of it, but after it had been quietly effected, how rarely he raised any objection, — indeed, how he sometimes quite rejoiced in it, and even on occasions plumed himself, taking the credit thereof. All this, I assured my husband, was but a repetition of my home experience. I used to insist that at the office he was the wife, and would often inquire after the health of his husband. He never had much to say at the time, but later I learned how he had thought the matter over, for he made an entire change in the management of the money matters both at the office and at home, and we have both been much happier ever since."

"If there is any part of this arrangement of which you would not mind speaking to others, I think it would help us very much," said Mrs. Hughes.

"Why, I had just as lief tell it all," said the Silent Lady, who had a slow, somewhat hesitating and timid manner. "We looked over our accounts, and decided just about what we needed each month for our living expenses. Then we divided these expenses; my husband took upon himself the ordering of fuel, the payment of rent, and other bills that seemed of an outside nature; while I took charge of all internal expenses, — servant-hire, grocery and meat bills, clothing for myself and children. There was provision made for sundries, and of this money I had much the larger share, because mine was to answer for the incidental expenses of the household as well as myself and children. The first of each month the money from the office was put in bank; the portion that we had agreed upon for my share was in my name, and my husband's was in his. Any money that was received at the office in addition to this was equally divided between us and placed to the credit of each, to spend or lay up as was thought best."

"I should think you might as well have been divided yourselves," said the Frivolous Person.

A hot flush and look of contempt flashed into the face of the Silent Member. Perhaps Mrs. Hughes feared an explosion of some kind, for she quickly said, —

"Oh, no, I don't think that follows; but, on the contrary, a much closer companionship between husband and wife. It seems to me that without some such arrangement no woman of any force or elevation of character could rest content. She would always, I think, harbor a sense of injustice, and be unable, even if his conduct in other regards were commendable, to give to her husband entire respect and love. But this source of irritation and resentment being removed, if other conditions are right, there may — as most of us, I hope, know by happy experience — exist the most perfect confidence and companionship. In our money affairs my husband and myself are entirely separate, and at the same time entirely united."

"That sounds like a fib," said the Sprightly Lady, "but it's built upon a deep underlying truth; I'm sure of it, if you say so, Mrs. Hughes."

Mrs. Hughes laughed. She was never offended, — indeed, few could be by the Sprightly One's mirth.

"Yes, it really is," she answered. "We are separate, as far as the right to interfere with each other is concerned; we are united, in that neither Mr. Hughes nor myself has ever made an investment or an expenditure of any importance without consultation. If we happened to be removed by distance at the time, we consulted by letter or telegram."

"After such an education in money matters, Mrs. Hughes, you would not be left in that helpless condition that so many women are when suddenly called to take charge of their husbands' affairs," said the Practical Person.

Mrs. Hughes's face changed. I had once seen a look of intense motherhood illuminate it; now it was as though it were filled with wifehood, — bereaved wifehood. It was a moment before she spoke; then she said slowly, and with some effort, "No, I should not be helpless in that respect."

Perhaps to relieve her for a moment, one of the Silent Members said : —

"My husband and I have a similar arrangement in money matters. Unfortunately, however, we are not ahead, so there is some difference. A few years ago we mismanaged dreadfully, as we can see now in looking back, and we have been behindhand ever since. This spring we came to the conclusion that we were not paying off our debts fast enough, and that although we kept accounts, the family expenses were running up higher than they ought to; so after much figuring we decided on the sum necessary for each month, and agreed to limit ourselves to this, foregoing every extra. Out of this amount a small sum was reserved for incidental private expenses. My husband takes his each month, and all the rest of the money we have to spend is put in the bank in my name. I pay every bill connected with the household, — in fact, manage all expenses. I have my check-book and bank-book, and I keep the strictest accounts, balancing the first of each month. My husband works very hard, and his business is so engrossing that he has very little time outside of his store. I dislike to have any part of this time taken for errands, and still more to add to his already heavily-taxed mind the care of remembering such errands; so, as I could very well attend to these matters, and especially as attending to them would give me a feeling of independence and a most useful knowledge, I proposed to undertake it, and he was glad enough to be relieved."

"There are many ways of regulating this matter," said Mrs. Hughes; "but the result is much the same, if that one main idea is kept in mind, that the money belongs to the wife just as much as to the husband, not by courtesy, not by gift, but by right of her having earned it."

"I think," said Dolly, "the hardest families to arrange this matter in are those where they are not ahead, and perhaps are a little in debt, and where they never know what to count on, — the income varying so that they can only plan and spend as the money actually comes into their hands."

"Yes, there are many in that lamentable state," said Mrs. Hughes, "where the necessarily uncomfortable position of the wife is aggravated by the lack of recognition of her rights. Such a lady was talking to me on this subject lately. She said, 'My husband is extremely economical. He really spends very little on himself, but whenever he does spend he has only to take the money from his pocket without asking any one; but I often suffer for the want of a dollar when I know I could have it, because I can't bear to go and ask for it.' I don't know what men think of such things, but to me they seem shamefully unjust. In the case I have mentioned, as in most families where the means are limited, the wife is more than earning her share. She is not only trying to perform her duties as wife and mother, but she is also taking upon herself the duties of servant besides. Her life is necessarily a very hard one, and certainly should not lack the comfort which a recognition of her commonest rights would give."

"Oh, Mrs. Hughes, it seems to me you're making much ado about nothing! I'm thankful we don't have any such system in our household — accounts, and all that. Why, it would drive me wild!" said the Frivolous Person. "When I want money," she continued, "I say so; and as I don't have to earn it, all I get is just so much gain. I have credit at some of the largest stores, too. My husband makes a terrible fuss over the bills sometimes; but then I cry a little, and we make up, — tears will cover a multitude of sins, you know;" and she laughed gayly at her own *naïveté* and adroitness.

I really felt relieved when Dolly followed up this folly by saying, —

"Don't you think, Mrs. Hughes, that women themselves are mainly answerable for their wrongs?"

"In most cases I do. I earnestly believe that when women entertain a more dignified and enlightened view of their rights and position, the greater part of these wrongs will melt away."

"How noble it would be for the men to step forward gratuitously, and do the handsome thing by us!" said the Sprightly Lady. "But we must n't look for masculine angels, I suppose."

"I don't know about that," said Dolly; "masculine angels are the only kind on record, I believe."

"Yes, but they were all busy with affairs celestial. I never heard of one's coming to this wicked world for more than a very brief call," the Sprightly Lady insisted.

Mrs. Hughes smiled.

"I would n't advise any one to wait for a

gratuitous settlement," she said. "I think the safer way is for every woman to give this subject careful thought, and then to take such steps as she decides her individual case demands. I really think that most men — all, I am sure, who have any manliness and sense of honor — will remedy these evils when their attention is really called to them. There are men who are incurably mean and dishonorable in this regard. Only lately my husband was talking to some one, and telling him of the arrangements we had made with respect to money matters; and this was his reply: 'I would n't give my wife so much rope for a good deal.' Had any one told this man that it was not a case of giving, but merely a question as to whether or not he would defraud his wife of her lawful share of the family earnings, he might have been shocked. But I think, as has been suggested, that more frequently the blame lies mainly with the wife. We have all of us heard women jest about rifling their husbands' pockets, and laughingly tell how they made a dollar or two out of them on some occasion; we have heard women tell how much they manage to save for themselves out of the allowance paid them by their husbands for household purposes. All I have to say is, that if women choose to accept, in their own houses, the position of a hired housekeeper, they must never complain at the results of such acceptance."

"I think the position is even inferior to that of a housekeeper, Mrs. Hughes," said Dolly, "for all hired housekeepers receive a salary, and have it paid at stated times; whereas many wives have to ask for a little money every now and then, and receive it as a sort of gift."

"Yes, that is true," said Mrs. Hughes, "or else steal it out of their husbands' pockets, or out of the money allowed them for the expenses of the household."

"Steal it!" said the Frivolous One, tossing her head. "I must say, Mrs. Hughes, you use strong language."

"There can be no half-way opinion in this matter; either a woman regards the money earned at office or store as belonging to herself as much as to her husband, or else she regards it as entirely his. If the latter case were true, she would have no right to a dollar without his consent, and whatever she took in any other way would be stolen. So all women who hold the latter view — as those must who talk about making any sum out of their husbands — must debase their consciences when they take money unknown to him who, in their eyes, is the lawful owner of such money."

"This is laying on color with startling liberality," sighed the Sprightly Lady. "Some of us will have to turn Catholic forthwith and borrow five cents of our husbands to buy an indulgence from the Pope."

"Supposing a woman earns money outside of her household," said the Practical Person, "do you think she ought to share it with her husband?"

"Certainly," said Mrs. Hughes. "As I said before, I regard husband and wife as two members of a firm, the time and abilities of each belonging to that firm. We know that the employment, by one of a firm, of his time and capacity for the making of money which he fails to divide, has been justly regarded as dishonest. I lately saw in the 'Nation' what I thought a very proper complaint, — that the law in a certain State had exceeded the limits of justice, in exempting the property of a married woman from liability for ordinary household debts, or even for her own maintenance. Again, the law is such that if a man proves vicious or worthless, and repudiates all debts, even though his wife may have money in her hands, she cannot be held responsible for them, — not even for such as pertain to the family living. Of course we can all see the intended beneficence of these laws; for in many cases, where the husband dies or proves worthless, the wife is left in a most helpless condition, and whatever money she may be able to realize from the sale of her furniture, or from any other source, is rarely sufficient to supply her own and her children's daily wants. A change in this particular law affecting a woman's relationship to the family debts would involve cruel suffering, and well-nigh as great injustice as the holding of a housekeeper responsible for such debts, unless there were also laws properly affecting a woman's relationship to the family means. When good laws on the latter point are enacted, and the monetary relationship between husband and wife becomes what it should be, it seems to me that the law would be perfectly just in holding the wife responsible for the family debts equally with the husband. She should know the strength and weakness of her income, and not incur more than she could meet, excepting, of course, in cases of actual destitution. I believe either a man or a woman is held guiltless for going beyond their means, to prevent physical suffering. In connection with this subject, I would like to say that it has always seemed to me that, in cases where the wife has held her lawful position with regard to money matters, and has means, either from life insurance or any other source, to pay the family debts, she would be most dishonorable to repudiate them."

"Oh, dear me!" sighed the Frivolous Young Person. "All this makes my brains whirl!"

I bent forward here with a longing to suggest to her that she mistook the rush of air in a cavity for the whirling of brains.

"Do you think, Mrs. Hughes," continued the Frivolous One, "that men and women are equal?"

Mrs. Hughes smiled.

"I am rather inclined to that opinion," she said, "though when I see some small, narrow men, and some noble women, my belief is a trifle shaken. We must not, however, dwell upon such points. We have to-day taken up some apparently irrelevant subjects, but they have seemed to me closely connected with our legitimate theme, — the management of servants. It is impossible to discuss that subject broadly and thoroughly without touching upon several others, just as it is impossible fully to discuss the troubles of the stomach without treating at some length those of the liver, the heart, and several other organs. But one thing is quite certain," Mrs. Hughes added, rising rather abruptly, after a glance at her watch, "we shall have to postpone not only kindred topics, but servant-girls themselves, until another meeting, for we have, I see, exceeded our time."

"Yes," said the Sprightly One, "I must

hasten away. What you said about half of a married woman's earnings belonging to her husband is pricking me terribly. I confess to having been scandalously corrupt. Week before last I made a nickel off the rag-man, and I did n't give Billy his two and a half cents. I must run home and divvy up ere I place my dishonest head upon a pillow."

CHAPTER VIII.

THE SERVANTS' SIDE.

"IT occurred to me the other day," said Mrs. Hughes, when the ladies were once more assembled, "that we had done a great deal of talking on our side, and but little on the servants',—I mean with regard to their lawful privileges."

"I think they have too many privileges now," observed the Imitation Millionnaire.

"I should say they had!" exclaimed the Frivolous Lady. "For my part, I scarcely dare say my soul's my own, to my cook."

"They have both too many and too few privileges, it seems to me," said Mrs. Hughes. "In some families they are allowed to be too familiar, and take undue liberties, while at the same time their lawful rights are disregarded. I believe in granting them every possible privilege that does not interfere with the proper performance of their work, or with a proper conception of their position."

"I agree with you there," said Dolly. "I

think their work is very disagreeable and hard, and they need every possible comfort."

"Oh, they don't regard their work as we would," said the Practical Lady; "they are much stronger than we are, and they are used to it, too."

"I think we are too apt to ease our consciences with that thought," persisted Dolly. "I know I used to; but last fall one of my servants taught me a lesson. She had lived with me several months, and I liked her very much. After a while, however, I noticed that she was growing dull and listless, and did not seem to take much pains with her work. All at once she told me that she must leave, to attend her sister's wedding; and she added that when she came back to the city she and this sister were going to dress-making. I talked with her awhile, and after asking a number of questions, I found that they had no definite arrangements made, no promise of work, but had decided, at random, as it were, to make dresses for a living. I told her that she could not earn as much as by doing housework, and that the work would be much less healthful; that in order to earn her board, lodging, and even less than her wages came to weekly right through the year, she would have to sew very hard. But what I said did n't seem to make much impression on her; and at last, attracted by her manner, I said, 'Mary, you are tired of housework.' I never shall forget the weary way in which she looked at me as she turned and said, 'Oh, I am so tired of it!' I felt very badly, for I wanted my servants to be happy, and to have as comfortable a life as possible. I asked her if there was any one particular thing more than another in her work that seemed hard. I hoped I could discover some especial evil and remedy it; but she did not particularize. I encouraged her to talk freely with me, for I wanted to learn from her; and she went on to say that it seemed to her as if her days were made up of a ceaseless round of dish-washing, scrubbing, dusting, sweeping, and cooking, not to mention the washing and ironing. There was no end to the work, and not much escape from it. If she went out any afternoon she had first to wash the dishes, and then hurry back to prepare a meal. She said she had been doing housework for several years, and she always noticed that after a girl had kept at it long she broke down, and then she was of no use to herself or any one else. I saw that it would be out of my power to enhearten her by talking, so I decided that the best thing for her to do was to try a change. I told her that she might think best to return to housework after she had rested awhile. Sure enough she did, after she had been gone two months and had tried various kinds of work. She heard I was going to dismiss the servant I had engaged in her place, and she came to see if I would take her back again. I gladly did, for she was a good girl, and I told her very frankly that I had never forgotten her talk with me, and that it had led me to make some important changes in my work, so that I felt I could offer a girl a better place than I had heretofore had for her."

"What changes did you make?" asked the Sprightly Lady. "I shall immediately 'renergade' my household, as Mrs. Partington would say."

"For one thing, I tried to show her how, by the use of energy and system, she could accomplish her work in less time, and I let her see she would be the gainer by this. I made every effort to secure her evenings for her, and then —"

"Excuse me for interrupting you," said Mrs. Hughes, "but I do wish you would dwell on that point at greater length. I so often feel indignant at the great indifference so many mistresses seem to feel about their servants' evenings."

"It is n't always possible to give them their evenings," said the Practical Person.

"No, not always; there will come times, of course, when we must have their services then, but when their work is so arranged — or I could better say disarranged — as to demand almost every evening, I think injustice is done them if they are not warned of this in their engagement, — and more than that, if they are not paid for night work. I think there are very few clerks so employed who are not paid accordingly; and a servant should be."

"I suppose, then, Mrs. Hughes," laughed the Practical Person, "if you called on a servant to pass water in the evening, you would raise her wages."

"Certainly," said the Sprightly Lady; "a nickel a drink!"

Mrs. Hughes laughed, but she was not to be shaken.

"No," she said, "I was not referring to any such trifling service as the answering of a doorbell or bringing a glass of water, — though I can say this, that at my house we call on the servants as little as possible in the evening; but there are many families where the dinner-hour is such that the cook could not possibly clear away everything before nine o'clock. In other households the hour set for dinner is reasonable enough, — six, it may be, — but the gentleman of the house is so irregular that though the servant occasionally has her evenings, generally she does not."

"But, Mrs. Hughes," objected a Silent Member, "supposing a man's business is such that he cannot come promptly to his meals; we know that doctors can't keep regular hours."

"I think that such people ought to pay an extra price to their servants, or else offer extra daytime privileges to compensate them for the loss of their evenings."

"I suppose, Mrs. Hughes, you think people ought to take dinner in the middle of the day, but we prefer to dine at night," said the Millionnaire, with a stylish sigh.

"We dine at night also," quietly replied Mrs. Hughes. "Two o'clock used to be our hour. Now, however, Mr. Hughes's business permits him to make it half-past five. We rarely vary a moment in sitting down, and as the waitress helps to clear away the dishes, all the work is finished by seven o'clock."

"Supposing you kept no waitress, what then?" asked the Practical Person.

"Before I kept a waitress, or had a butler's pantry, I allowed the cook to leave all the dining-room dishes, china, glass, and silver, neatly piled on a small side-table in the dining-room. These dishes were out of our sight as we sat in the parlor, and could be quickly washed in the morning. It was not, of course, my chosen way, but it was the best I could do then, and it seemed to me more just than to take my servants' own time to put my dining-room in perfect order."

"Supposing, Mrs. Hughes, you had had a tardy husband, what would have become of Biddy then, poor thing?" asked the Sprightly Lady.

Here I shrank farther into my retreat, for I felt that these remarks were becoming disturbingly personal. I was tardy myself occasionally.

"I had that domestic grievance once," said Mrs. Hughes, with a smile; "but I sat down to dinner promptly."

"Was Mr. Hughes sent to bed without his dinner?" inquired the Sprightly Lady, with an air of concern.

"No; but when he came I laid the matter before him —"

"What, — the lecture, or the dinner?" asked the Sprightly One.

"'Both, your Majesty!'" laughed Mrs. Hughes; "for I waited on him myself, and I took care that my discourse should follow a good dinner. In fact, I did not say anything the first time or two, and at last, when I did speak of the servants' rights and hardships in this respect, Mr. Hughes had the manliness and good sense to see the justice of it all, and as there was no real cause for his tardiness, he corrected it, very much to the benefit of his health, as well as to our servants' comfort."

"But, Mrs. Hughes," persisted the Practical Person, "some men cannot be regular — doctors, for instance."

"I think most irregular men could improve if they tried hard enough, even doctors. The trouble with such is, that because they are obliged to be somewhat lax, they learn to look upon their irregularity lightly, and often practise it unnecessarily, not realizing how much they are adding to the toils of the servants and the cares of the housekeeper. At the risk of repeating myself again and again, I must say that I think servants, as a class, are very hardly dealt with, and I earnestly believe that more competence on the part of their mistresses, added to more justice and kindness, would almost entirely abolish these servant troubles, the outcry about which rings from shore to shore of our country."

"It might be more discreet, Mrs. Hughes, to lay the blame on the servants, since they are not here and cannot fight back," said the Sprightly Lady.

"More discreet, and likewise more cowardly," said Dolly.

"I think the servants have been blamed too much already," Mrs. Hughes continued. "They have faults enough, without being made to bear those of other people."

"I fear, Mrs. Hughes," observed the Imitation Millionnaire, with polite severity, "you would revolutionize our whole service."

"I wish she might," responded one of the Silent Members, whose face had a careworn look. "I would n't care who was blamed, myself or my servant, so the remedy was pointed out."

"Many women," said Mrs. Hughes, "complain that their lot in life is needlessly made much harder than the lot of men. You can look about you in any assemblage, and you will see the word 'injustice' written on the faces of a large number of the women. And yet, when women have to deal with women, they aggravate rather than decrease this very element of injustice. For my part, I never could see why a great number of day laborers in our country should earn from one to two dollars a day, and have their working-time reduced from twelve to ten and from ten to eight hours, while the large mass of working-women are expected to be on duty from five or six in the morning until nine or ten at night, and in many families to be actively employed most of that time,— Sundays included, — for the sum of thirty or forty cents a day."

"And their board, Mrs. Hughes; you forget that," said the Practical Person.

"Yes," said Mrs. Hughes; "but in many families the board is only worthy of being forgotten. No; deny or evade it as we will, there is clearly a wrong in this difference between the service of men and women. We are greatly indebted to our servants; they save us both time and strength, and take much that is hard and disagreeable out of our lives. But our return for all this is most meagre."

"Well, Mrs. Hughes, if your ideas were carried out — I mean, if we had to pay women as much as men — most of us would have to do without servants," said the Practical Person.

"I am reminded just here of one of Mr. Beecher's sermons, in which he dwelt at length upon the care of the slave which was enjoined by the Lord in olden times. He said that it was not every one who could afford to keep slaves under those conditions; and that it was just so in our country, — the moment that slave-holders were compelled to do full justice to their slaves, that moment slavery became too expensive a luxury."

"Would you then abolish servants, Mrs. Hughes?" queried the Imitation Millionnaire, in such icy tones that I felt she ought to be put in the oven for an hour or two.

"No, I don't think that would be necessary; but I would have them very differently treated.

A lady friend of mine was almost offended with me when she learned that I was paying my cook what she termed too high wages. She said that I was inflicting a wrong upon other ladies by so doing. I know of a lady who is wealthy, and who pays her cook but three dollars a week, not because she can afford no more, but because she takes her stand upon high moral grounds, and thinks that she has no right to unsettle service by paying extravagant wages. Some time ago I read in a magazine a short article on the servant question, which contended that it was unjust to fix upon one average price, and pay this to the skilled and the unskilled alike; and with this sentiment I heartily agree."

"But, Mrs. Hughes," exclaimed the Practical Person, with some excitement, "do you see where all this is going to lead us?"

"That is a secondary matter beside the question, 'Is it right?'" answered Mrs. Hughes.

"Certainly," said the Sprightly Lady; "if it's time to take a bath, don't go to poking a stick in the water, to see whether you're going to alight on rock or sand; just hop in, head first."

Everybody laughed here, particularly those ladies whose faces expressed opposition to the new suggestions; but Mrs. Hughes proceeded quietly:—

"As I said before, I don't think that justice and kindness would abolish service. I believe, however, that it would be improved thereby. It is true that many, perhaps the large majority of families, could not afford to employ skilled labor; but in that respect I don't think they would be any worse off than they are now. There are, and probably always will be, many young, inexperienced girls, whose strength and time would be of aid. Various arrangements might be made with such servants; if they were docile, and reasonably bright, they might be paid a small sum — perhaps a dollar a week — in addition to their board, for three months; then, if they had improved sufficiently to warrant it, two dollars a week for another three months. By this time they ought to become very competent servants."

"And this would be about the time they would murmur 'By-by' to the poor little poverty-stricken instructress, and pass over to some ten-dollar-a-week lady," said the Sprightly Member.

"Yes, indeed!" murmured an indignant chorus.

"That could be prevented by arranging that the girl should continue her service for moderate wages — three dollars a week, perhaps — for six months after she became competent."

"How could you hold her?" asked a Silent Member.

"That might be managed by making a written agreement with her when she first came, and paying her but a small part of her wages until the end of the year. For myself, though, I would prefer to draw up the contract and merely trust to her honor to keep it. I have again and again trusted to a servant's honor in matters of this kind, and in an experience of some years have rarely ever been disappointed."

"What of this domestic lady, after she becomes skilled and has served her six months?" asked the Sprightly One.

"I cannot pretend to set positive wages, but I can give it as my opinion that skilled service, instead of receiving too much at present, does not receive enough. Compensation would, I think, be the key to the difficulty arising from the payment of very high wages by the wealthy few. Probably a large number, even of those who are comparatively well off, could not afford to give such wages, but they might give somewhat more than they do, if they denied themselves needless things; and this, with the addition of many privileges in the way of time not granted by those who paid more, would probably always insure them good servants."

"Oh, my husband says it's all nonsense for a

woman to think of earning as much as a man!" exclaimed the Frivolous Lady. "He says that they lack permanency, and so they are not of as much account. He says that the moment a woman is well broken in to any business she flies off and marries."

"That is largely true in some occupations, and must, of course, impair the value of female service, but I cannot believe that it applies here. I think that we could find as many female as male servants who had remained in the same place a number of years; and yet it often happens that a man will be paid more, even in this capacity, than a woman. A friend of mine in a distant city told me that the highest price paid to a cook was from seventeen to twenty dollars a month, while a coachman in the same place received as much as forty dollars; and his work was seldom so hard, and, indeed, called for less knowledge and skill. Such things are unjust."

"But, Mrs. Hughes," exclaimed the Practical Person, "surely you would n't have us pay girls forty dollars a month!"

"No, I think those wages too high, excepting in very rare cases; but I also think it wrong to pay them to coachmen."

"Mrs. Hughes, I think you lose sight of some points in this question," said the Practical Person. "When men earn two and three dollars a day as laborers, it is not in some situation which they can render comparatively permanent if they will, but for what might be called odd jobs usually; and although some of the most fortunate do have steady work the year through at such rates, they are not in the majority by any means. Then, again, I know that in the payment of their employees, business men often make a distinction between single and married men, paying the higher wages to the latter."

"I bear all this in mind, I think, and for that, among other reasons, do not advocate paying our servants two or three dollars a day; but all you have just said does not argue away the injustice of paying single men forty dollars a month and their board, when they are employed as coachmen, while the cook, and also the laundress, in the same family, receive but twenty dollars monthly. No; we cannot deny that there is a wrong here which must needs be righted some time or other. Look at the cases where married women are hired by the job. Some of us grumble a little if we have to pay a woman a dollar and a half for standing at an ironing-board all day. It does not matter if she understands her business and does up our clothes beautifully, we think she is well paid for it; and if she finishes her work by four or five in the afternoon we feel quite injured, and tell how Mrs. Smith or Mrs. Jones once had a laundress who came at seven and worked till seven, for a dollar and a quarter. A shame on Mrs. Smith or Mrs. Jones, I say, to take a working-woman's time, strength, and skill, without paying her for them! No dollar and a quarter ever paid for eleven or twelve hours laundry-work, if the work was at all well done! I am ashamed of my sex whenever I hear of such things. And there are sewing-girls who are wronged, too. How much has been written to induce people to hire them for seventy-five cents or a dollar a day! We would think a dollar and a half very high, and two dollars out of the question, even if they took but one meal at our houses."

"Mrs. Hughes," said one of the Silent Members, upon whose face the word "injustice" was certainly written, if ever it was written upon any woman's countenance, "women are not wholly to blame in this matter, for the majority of housekeepers have so little money allowed them for household expenses, and have so little strength left after attending to the demands of a number of children, that they have to get their work done for the least possible amount."

"There is both comfort and humiliation in this thought, — comfort in the hope that when women have their rights they will deal more honorably by their own sex, and humiliation in the knowledge that they are so deeply wronged now."

"Oh, really, Mrs. Hughes, men can't always help it!" exclaimed the Sprightly Lady. "Don't chastise the poor fellows with scorpions when they don't deserve it. Some of them are as poor as Job's celebrated fowls, you know."

" Yes, I know that; but there is nevertheless a wrong, — one that we cannot take up now, as it has but a remote connection with the servant question, and is, indeed, difficult to deal with at any time. But I can say this much, and then return to the main subject of our discussion. Unless sickness or some unlooked-for calamity has made a great and unexpected change in the aspect of home affairs, there is always a wrong involved when women are so heavily burdened with cares that they cannot order aright their own lives and those of others over whom they have control. I had intended merely to touch upon this question of servants' wages, inasmuch as very little that is definite can be said upon the subject. In my experience I have found, even since my income justified me in giving the highest wages, that, except in rare cases, where the value of the servant is unquestionable, it is better to begin with the payment of moderate wages, promising an increase at the rate of half a dollar a week, perhaps, every few months, if the girl's acquirements should justify it. Housework is, in many respects, so variable, — different families have such diverse ways of doing their work, — that a girl almost always has much to learn in a new place; and for this reason, and also because the increase of wages gives her an incentive to remain, it is wise to adopt this plan. I have generally done so, telling the servant, upon her engagement, when I would raise her wages, and to what sum, that she might know just what to expect. Indeed, I have the articles of our agreement very plainly drawn up, and in some cases put down in writing."

"Mrs. Hughes," said Dolly, "do you object to a girl's asking a great many questions when she comes to apply for a place?"

"Certainly not. I ask many myself as to her knowledge and references. Why should she not want to know about her work, — to know what she is undertaking? Of course a girl may make her inquiries in an insolent manner, and in such a case I would reject her; or she may show, by the style of her inquiries, that she is one of those who will go just so far and not an inch farther, in responding to necessary demands, and I always reject any one who betrays such a disposition; but I have for years past had very little trouble either in engaging or keeping servants. Sickness, marriage, or removal of their families, have been the only causes of my changing, or their leaving me."

"Do you tell a girl all your requirements upon engaging her?" asked Dolly.

"No, that would be impossible. I learn something of her abilities, and then after telling her of my few rules about the servants' table, their dress, and so on, I say something like this: 'You will find me very strict and particular in some things, but you will also find, I think, that I do not begrudge my servants any privilege or pleasure which it is possible for me to grant. Indeed, it would be a grief to me to learn that one of my maids was unhappy. I want you to have your pleasures, and will often be willing to put myself out considerably to give them to you. I shall do the very best I can by you, and I shall look to you to do the very best you can by me.'"

"At this point," said the Sprightly One, "they should begin to use their kerchiefs violently."

Mrs. Hughes laughed.

"No, they don't weep here, but they are nevertheless impressed by the idea that they are going to be justly and kindly treated. And if they are so treated, — if we constantly, by words, and by example, which is more powerful, set before them the value of honor and justice, — we shall find that, in the long run, they will treat us well also."

"Now we are upon the subject of servants' privileges," said Dolly, "what time do you allow them for their own, Mrs. Hughes?"

Mrs. Hughes was about to reply, when she suddenly glanced at the clock.

"Speaking of time," she said with a laugh, "reminds me that it is high time I held my peace for to-day."

"Let it be agreed, then, that servants are to have no time at all until we meet again and decide upon the proper quantity," said the Sprightly Lady; and with that, the Club adjourned.

CHAPTER IX.

SERVANTS' LEISURE TIME.

THE Sprightly Lady opened the next meeting by saying, in a tone of deep solicitude:
"Is it not almost time our poor servants had a vacation of some sort? They have been shut up for a week now."

"What time do you think we ought to give them, Mrs. Hughes?" asked Dolly, repeating herself, unlike Shakespeare.

"Well, I must say, I think the Club is taking a queer turn. I supposed we met to increase our privileges in dealing with these servants, but it seems we are here to increase theirs!" exclaimed the Frivolous Person.

"There are two sides to this matter, as there are to every right; it is only wrongs that are one-sided." Mrs. Hughes spoke almost severely, an unusual tone for her; but I think that the Frivolous Young Person had strained her patience. "As to the matter of a servant's time one can fix no rules, because the needs of different families are various; but I really think that they might have more time than is usually given them. It seems too bad to allow a servant but one afternoon during the week-days, and to expect her then to hurry home and get a dinner or supper. Sundays, too, families are often inconsiderate; they like a dinner in the middle of the afternoon, and the poor servant is unable to get out until near evening. We forget that most of us live a long way from the homes and churches of these girls, and much of their time is consumed in merely going and coming. I have often heard ladies express indignation at the unwillingness of servants to go far out of town; but we ought not to feel so. We would not like to live at a great distance from our friends, the churches, and the stores, if our leisure time was as limited as theirs. It is a poor comment upon our characters that such is the case, but we certainly do need to be often reminded of the fact that our servants are human beings. They have their needs as well as we, and one of these needs is pleasure, — recreation; and we should see to it that it is properly supplied."

"I don't believe in allowing servants to stay out after ten o'clock at night, nor in letting them take the door-key," said a Silent Member.

"Oh, I don't care how late they stay, so they do their work!" exclaimed the Millionnaire.

"I can't agree with that," said Dolly.

"No," said Mrs. Hughes. "I think we are largely responsible to God if our servants go to ruin in body or soul, and they might do so if we were thus careless about them. They are more than machines; and although the doing of our work is an important consideration, it is not the only one. Ten o'clock is, in many cases, a reasonable hour; but I often make exceptions. I tell my servants that it is not possible for them to sit up late nights and do their work properly the next day without injuring their health. They rarely ever are later than ten in going to bed when they go to church; but they attend a club-meeting once in a while, and then it is generally eleven, sometimes later, before they return. I think that if all ladies would consider their servants a little more, and on such evenings let them start out earlier, they would not have to stay so late; for my servants tell me that on account of the tardiness of the members in getting there, it is often half-past eight before the programme begins,— then comes a supper, and on some occasions a little dance."

"The gay Bridgets!" murmured the Sprightly Lady.

"Yes," continued Mrs. Hughes, "the young of most animals of which we have any knowledge like and need recreation; and though the reading of Baxter's 'Saint's Rest' may be sufficient for an aged Christian, it is not generally so for a young servant-girl. With regard to my servants' evenings, as I have often said, I have never yet felt that any wages we gave them was sufficient to pay for night work; but I have a continual oversight and authority over their night as well as their day, for the sake of their characters, just as many an employer has a knowledge of the manner in which his employee spends his leisure, and indeed some authority as well. I think I have my servants' confidence; they tell me where they are going, and the next day I always ask if they had a pleasant time, and am interested in hearing something of what went on. When they are out unusually late, I generally contrive to have them rest a little the next day and go to bed early the next night."

"I feel it's a mercy if they don't want to run out every night," said the Practical Person.

"I don't allow that, excepting in rare instances; for even if the places to which they went were all proper, I think it would be injurious to them to go out so much. Christmas week there is a great deal going on, and I let the servants dissipate a little, as do the rest of us. I like considerable gayety at that time myself, and I am anxious that the servants should have a good time. We all rest afterward."

"Do you have anything to say about your servants' evenings when they stay at home?" asked Dolly.

"I try to influence them to employ their time to advantage, — to do their mending and some of their plainer sewing (I let them use my machine), and I try to supply them with simple but improving reading."

"I think they must have a pretty good time in your house," said the Imitation Millionnaire, with the faintest, most fashionable trace of a sneer.

"I hope they do," answered Mrs. Hughes; "I should grieve to think I had an overworked or unhappy servant in the house."

"Do your servants never have to work nights?" asked a Silent One.

"Yes; in emergencies, such as times of sickness, or when I am preparing for a journey, I sometimes have to call on them, — or rather I should say they volunteer, for they seldom have to be asked. If they know I am in any extremity they appear at once. But if they do extra work for me, I generally compensate them by a present, or by some privilege — though not always; sometimes, for their sake, I accept their service as I would accept the service of a friend."

"Surely, Mrs. Hughes," exclaimed the Imitation Millionnaire, "you don't count your servants your friends!"

"Not in a social sense, but in the broader sense of humanity I do, and I trust I have proved myself their friend."

"Why, Mrs. Hughes," said the Frivolous Lady, "I have always heard that you were an aristocrat!"

"If that means I have strong feelings on the subject of caste, you have heard aright; but of that, perhaps, we had better speak at some other time."

"What about servants' company, Mrs. Hughes?" asked a Silent Lady.

"I always made my servants understand that their friends were welcome, out of working hours. On special occasions they have had the privilege of inviting several friends to take dinner with them."

"'High life below stairs'!" murmured the Sprightly Lady.

"And whenever any relatives or especial friends from another city came in to see them, they were allowed to invite them to stay to whatever meal was at hand."

"I think your kitchen must have been full of company half the time," said the Imitation Millionnaire.

"No, it was not. I think you would find, as

I have, that good servants appreciate but never abuse this privilege, and I never extend it to any others; in fact, I never keep any others. There is a point in connection with a servant's time of which I would like to speak. I once heard a friend complain bitterly because, after setting out her Sunday evening tea, she discovered that her servant was upstairs, instead of being out of the house, as she had supposed. She thought the girl ought to have come down and helped. This struck me as very unjust. Considering the fact that these employees of ours work for us seven days in the week, instead of six, as most others do, a certain amount of leisure is their right. Now, if instead of going out the girl prefers to take that time to sew or rest at home, I don't think I should call on her any more than if she were at the North Pole. I make this clear to my servants, telling them that if they wish to spend their leisure at home they will be just as uninterrupted, so far as my work is concerned, as if they were at the home of some friend."

"I think that many ladies are unreasonable and unjust toward their servants," said Dolly, with much force.

"There is no doubt of that," said Mrs. Hughes, "but the law of compensation finds them out. I know a number of mistresses who are really their servants' slaves in many ways. They have been unjust, unreasonable, and mean for so long that they have acquired a bad name among the girls, and their house is avoided. I think it must be mistresses of this sort whom I have occasionally seen at intelligence offices fairly begging girls to come to them, offering them all sorts of foolish indulgences, and so humbling themselves before them that they must have inspired a thorough contempt. These women were probably fresh from a long siege of trials which resulted from doing their own work, and were brought to the extremity of offering many unwise privileges, and more than that, of obeisance to these servants. When such people succeed in inducing girls to enter their service, they are forced to treat them as if they were glass, and might break at any moment. They tremble continually for fear they will leave; they scarcely dare have any company, and really live in a sort of reign-of-terror atmosphere in their own houses."

"'The way of the transgressor is hard,'" said the Sprightly Lady, wiping her eyes.

"It is, indeed," said Mrs. Hughes, with a smile; "and lest I may be forced to walk therein, I will bring my remarks to a close before I transgress upon your time, as I did at our last meeting."

CHAPTER X.

HONOR ABOVE AND BELOW STAIRS.

"MRS. HUGHES," said the Sprightly Lady, soon after the Club had assembled for its ninth meeting, "did you see that article the other day asking why shop-girls preferred to sew for three dollars a week instead of going out to service and earning two and a half, with board?"

"Yes; and I also saw a reply to it to-day, ostensibly written by a shop-girl."

"What did you think of it all?" queried Dolly.

"I thought there was both sense and nonsense in it. It would certainly have a good influence over mistresses, to bear constantly in mind the fact that their house is the only home their servants have as long as they live out. This idea, enforced by kindness and justice, would, I think, tend to produce a greater degree of comfort for the servants in all respects. But when it comes to any attempt to pull down the wall between the kitchen and the parlor, to abolish caste, and put the servant on a par with the family, I am strongly opposed to it; for, as far as I can see, little but evil would result to both employers and employees from such a course. Servants would imbibe many false ideas as to their position, and their needs of dress, and so on, — ideas more or less injurious to their time, means, and ultimately to their characters, — and certainly the family would degenerate in manners, if not in morals, from an intimate association with those as uncultured and ignorant as are the large majority of our servants. I confess I have no patience with any talk that aims at the abolition of caste; for it is time and strength wasted, or worse than wasted, since it puts pernicious ideas into the minds of the ignorant. The rank of shop-girl, though a degree or two higher than that of kitchen-maid, is nevertheless beneath that of lady, and — "

"Oh, Mrs. Hughes!" exclaimed a Silent Member, "I have been taught that whoever behaves well and possesses a fine character is a lady, whether she is found in the parlor of her own home, or earning her living at the wash-tub. I have been taught to respect true womanhood wherever it appears."

"It is a noble lesson," said Mrs. Hughes, with that gentle courtesy which was one of her strongest characteristics. "I wish we had all learned to reverence womanhood and manhood wherever found; to look up to humanity, and to feel that on the great questions of life we should all be as one family. But there are smaller matters, finer, nicer distinctions, certain graces of mind and manner, which a form of education, to which we give the name of culture, alone seems able to inculcate; and it is when I see one who combines such culture with the grand traits of true womanhood, that I feel I am privileged to behold a perfect lady. She would be a most extraordinary servant indeed, who could enter a parlor graced with such people and enjoy their social pleasures. What would be delightful to them would be very dull to her, and the amusements and conversation which would entertain and engage her, would give to ladies but small pleasure, if indeed they were not repelled thereby. It is a difficult matter, this of always bearing true womanhood and manhood in mind reverently; this of broadening our sympathies, enlarging our humanity, and yet never doing that foolish and wicked thing of forsaking our high estate, — selling our birthright of culture, of mental superiority, and descending to the masses, because we wish to illustrate a crude theory of equality."

"Ah, Mrs. Hughes!" exclaimed the Sprightly Lady, "I always knew you were an aristocrat."

"So am I," said the Frivolous Person. "Why, last week my husband said he wanted to bring a young man out to dinner with him. He praised him up to the skies, and said he was going to make his mark, and all that; but at the last moment I found out that his mother used to be my mother's seamstress, and I told my husband that if he invited him he 'd have to dine alone with him; I was n't going to sit down to dinner with any seamstress's son."

I saw Mrs. Hughes's face struggle to preserve its equanimity against an almost overwhelming feeling of scorn.

"I think this must have been the young man who dined with us to-day," she observed quietly.

"What! do you entertain such company?" exclaimed the Frivolous Person.

"Very rarely; for it is sadly true that one seldom has the privilege of meeting such a splendid fellow as this young man."

"But he used to be a tinner!" gasped the Frivolous Young Person. "I really did n't know that at first, and of course you did n't know it."

"Oh, yes, I knew that and much more about him."

The Frivolous Person had nothing further to say, but her face expressed the fact that she had but a small opinion of Mrs. Hughes, from that moment.

"Then a man's occupation makes no difference to you. For my part, I confess I have always had a weakness for the professions," sighed the Imitation One.

"Oh, yes," replied Mrs. Hughes, "I think that in the long run we may confidently expect to find a certain class of people in a certain occupation. But there are striking exceptions to this rule, and if we do not wish to lose an opportunity, not only for doing right but also for enlarging our natures, and improving our minds as well as characters, we should keep a watch for just such exceptions, and recognize them heartily when they appear. But I must not digress; this subject of aristocracy bears upon the servant question only in a limited degree."

"I think it bears upon it forcibly, for I find that most of these foreigners come over to this country with an idea that in America all stand on an equality," said the Imitation Member.

"Yes," answered Mrs. Hughes, "and this idea is not confined to servants alone. A friend of mine who was travelling in Sweden met there a lady of high rank, and was questioned by her about America. This Swedish lady insisted that she would not like to live here. 'Oh, I could not live there!' she exclaimed, 'for my servants and family would all be on an equality!' and it was almost impossible to make her understand that ideas of caste obtained, even in our new country. I have again and again talked to servants on this subject."

"What do you say to them?" asked Dolly.

"Perhaps the easiest answer to that question," said Mrs. Hughes, "would be to tell of a servant I once had; and this story will also illustrate a statement I made as to the strength of servant-girls' sense of honor. I engaged this girl, on a two weeks' trial, as nurse. She had been highly recommended by her last mistress, the wife of a lieutenant, who had, as I afterward learned, foolishly indulged her, and only parted with her because she was to leave the city and could not take her. Bridget was a smart, pleasant girl, — Irish on her mother's side and Hollander on her father's. I saw she would not do. To begin with, she came to the front door when she first arrived, and although I lived in a small house then, my front and side or back doors were as distinct as now. She often went up and down the front stairs, and she was constantly attempting to talk with me with the easy familiarity of an old friend. She spoke to and of the children in the same way, and when she came into the drawing-room at night to take them away to bed, she would enter into a conversation with them right before the family, arguing about their going, and so on. She had sense enough to see that all these ways were displeasing to us, but not sense enough to change them. At the end of two days I told her that I saw she would not do for the place, and she told me she would not care to stay. She talked very freely with me, and as she spoke pleasantly and without impertinence, I listened to all she had to say. She told me she would not be willing to live in any place where she would not be treated as one of the family. I then told her of the mistake she and many other foreigners made, with regard to this country; told her that ideas of caste were as strong here as elsewhere, though, on account of the absence of titles, less clearly defined. I told her that if she wished to be received on terms of equality with a family of education and refinement, there was a possible course open to her, if she possessed great natural ability; but that such a course meant very hard work — the hard study necessary for self-education. If she used every spare hour to study and improve herself, she might hope, in the course of time, to take a very different position from that which she then occupied; but unless she was willing to perform the work, she must not expect to reap the reward, — in plainer words, as long as she was greatly inferior to her employers in education and general culture, she must not expect to be received as an equal. I told her, furthermore, that all did not have to toil so unremittingly as she would, in order to obtain these privileges, for some were born to them; that is, refinement of nature and manner, and an inclination toward education, came to some as a birthright, but with this, a certain amount of mental work must be performed, or even the possessor of such natural advantages failed to hold his place in the highest circle. Furthermore, I told her that if she felt disinclined to toil in that way, in order to obtain such social advantages, it was possible for her to earn an honest living, and win the respect of her employers, without such mental labor. I told her that the pride that prevented her from taking her proper position in the social scale was false; true pride she should not be without, and I thought she did possess much of that. I bade her cling to the pride which kept her honest, the pride that kept her virtuous, and also to cultivate that pride in her work which made her strive toward perfection in its performance,— that pride which forbade her to take from an employer a dollar which she could not feel she had truly earned. Such pride would greatly aid her to lead a respected and happy life; but the foolish pride which made her covet and even insist upon social privileges which she was unfitted to receive, was unworthy of respect, — of aught, indeed, but scorn.

"I know not what effect these words may have had upon her later. Possibly there came a time when their truth was made clearer to her; but when I spoke there was no sign that she saw any reason to change her views or desires. It was decided that we should part, and she remarked that at the end of two weeks I would doubtless have found somebody to take her place; and to this I assented. That week, Friday, I let her go out, and upon her return she told me that a lady living next door to her former mistress wanted to engage her for the same price I was paying, and had but one child, instead of two, for her to take charge of; but if she took this place she must go at once, as the lady was ill and could not wait. She told me that she had promised to go to her Monday. I said, 'You are not free to go, Bridget.' This surprised her; but I went on: 'Did you not engage yourself to me for two weeks?' 'Yes'm, but I did n't know as I promised to stay that long.' 'To what did the engagement amount, then? If you were free to leave me as soon as you found another place, then I must have been free to discharge you as soon as I found another girl; and in that case your engagement to stay with me two weeks, and mine to keep you two weeks, was mere nonsense. The only exception we made to the binding of the contract was some very flagrant act either on your part or mine. But nothing of that sort has occurred, so I am bound to keep you till the end of two weeks, and you are bound to stay, unless we both agree to part before then.' She replied that all that was something she had not thought of, and she considered herself free to go and take that place. I said, 'Bridget, there is no law to prevent you from walking out of my house to-night, save the law of honor. You are bound by your word.' She answered me, as earnestly as I spoke, 'Mrs. Hughes, I never told a falsehood in my life.' I said that I hoped she never would, but that she could not leave me before her time expired, unless I was willing to have her do so, without breaking her word. She said it was not very pleasant for her to feel that she was bound. I told her that every contract was binding, and that no business could be carried on without contracts; that whenever a girl went to a place there was a verbal contract made, she agreeing to do certain work, and the mistress agreeing to give certain privileges and pay certain wages. No business could be carried on, I told her, if people universally broke their contracts. Because many people did so, there was much trouble in the business world. I also explained to her that no contract could bind one side alone, and that in our own particular case I was not free to take another girl unless I kept her and continued her wages also. For that reason, I said, I had not yet begun to look for a girl; for I did not suppose one would be willing to delay coming to me so long, and I did not wish to be paying two for the same work. I saw signs of her yielding, but she maintained that she did not want to lose a good place, — that she would rather lose all her wages from me. I replied, 'Your wages, Bridget, are the least of what you would lose if you left me in defiance of your promise; you would lose your character as an honorable girl.' I assured her that I should be very sorry to have her forfeit a good place on my account, and that I would take every pains to secure a girl so that she could leave me in time to go to this lady, but that in my health I did not feel able to be left with but one servant.

"I applied immediately to two intelligence offices, and spoke to a number of my friends of my need; but until the next Wednesday I did not succeed in procuring a suitable nurse. Bridget had not said she would stay, but in my own mind I had little doubt of it, so strong had I always found this sense of honor and justice in the minds of respectable servants. When I came to settle with her on the following Wednesday, I told her that her course had won my respect, and that I hoped she would always so live as to compel the respect of all who dealt with her. I paid her up to the time she left, although she said I need only pay her for one week. I told her also that if she had lost that place and wished to stay with me till the end of the two weeks, I was bound to keep her and pay her the two weeks' wages, and that I would do so cheerfully. But she thought she might possibly be able to get that place, or if not, she could take another. She told me she wanted to thank me for the lesson I had taught her; that I had impressed her with the feeling that I would treat her with the strictest kindness and justice; and more than that, I had led her to see a meaning in an engagement which she had never thought of before."

"I should think such a servant as that could instruct many mistresses in the code of honor," said a Silent Member. "I have known ladies who needed a girl for a few weeks only, during the vacation of the regular servant or something of that kind, to engage one without telling her that the place was only temporary."

"Yes, I have known of that and other dishonorable actions on the part of mistresses; and when I contrast these things with the conduct of many servants I have had, I feel as if honor had fled to the basement."

"Why, really, Mrs. Hughes," said the Imitation Millionnaire, "I think you are rather severe; for my part, I cannot see that a mistress is bound to specify the length of time when she engages a servant."

"No, she can hardly do so," returned Mrs. Hughes, "for the term of engagement must be regulated by many unforeseen circumstances. But a lady who deliberately withholds anything which she has reason to believe would cause the girl to refuse the place, is acting dishonorably. Few girls who are worth having would be willing to undertake to learn the duties of a new situation, to say nothing of the trouble and expense of moving their baggage, and the possible loss of a good permanent place, just for a few weeks' time."

"But, Mrs. Hughes," said the Sprightly Lady, with an unusually serious face, "a mistress may not know whether or not her place will be permanent. If her regular servant has gone off on a vacation, she can't be sure she'll return."

"That is true; but if she is wishing her to return, and hoping that she will, she does very wrong to engage a girl without telling her of the circumstances."

"I guess she wouldn't get any girl if she did," said the Practical Person.

"And that ought, in itself, to be sufficient to prove the dishonesty of withholding the information. When we gain any advantage by keeping back facts that bear upon it closely,—facts which would, if known, prevent the transaction from being made, — we are acting dishonorably. We might as well withhold the fact of a doubtful title on a piece of land we were trying to sell, on the ground that we could not otherwise get rid of it, and then expect to be considered honest, as to withhold from a servant we are trying to engage the fact that the place she supposes may be comparatively permanent is in all probability temporary. Let us turn the tables, and see how the matter will look, for we are all so selfish that we see justice and right more clearly when we are the claimants. Suppose we engage a girl in good faith, and after a few weeks, just as we have accustomed her to her duties, and are beginning to rest from our labors, we are told that she is going back to her old place; that the family have been out of town, and she had only come to us so as to be earning something during their absence. Would we not be indignant with her? And would we not immediately exclaim,

'Why did n't you tell me this? You knew I would never have engaged you for a few weeks!' I have no doubt that the very ladies who themselves are capable of such conduct would be quite outraged if thus treated, and would inveigh against these 'lying domestics,' — for certainly a lie acted equals a lie spoken, and so they would consider."

"But, Mrs. Hughes, do you think a lady ought to do without help while her servant takes a vacation?" asked a Silent Member.

"Certainly, if she cannot honestly obtain help; but I think that she can. I have for years been in the habit of giving my servants vacations, and I have had but little trouble in obtaining substitutes. They generally see to this, and sometimes a friend, not ordinarily living out, takes the place; and sometimes it is a girl just arrived in the city. They almost always contrive to find some one, if need be, who is willing to come for a few weeks."

"To recur to the shop-girls again, Mrs. Hughes," said Dolly, "I think that they might find places as congenial to their sense of dignity as the shop, and better for their health and purse. There are a large number of families, in the middle class, whose means would not allow them to pay high wages to servants. I should think that in such houses bright shop-girls might find real homes, where by joining with the mistress in doing the work they could receive as much as two dollars and a half a week, and at the same time enjoy the privileges of the members of the family."

"Undoubtedly such arrangements are often made, and it is a pity they are not still more common, for they would greatly lighten the cares of housekeepers, and provide healthful occupation, small wages, and pleasant homes for a large class of working-girls. In the article I mentioned reading this morning, the writer speaks as if almost all the shop-girls in Chicago lived at their own homes, where they had no board to pay, and where they enjoyed all the comforts and privileges of petted members of a small but comfortable household. The picture was quite alluring, but I doubt its fidelity. It is possible, barely possible, that Chicago is exceptionable in this respect; but in other cities we too often hear a cry of overworked and underpaid shop-girls, who are driven to crime for mere support, and some of us have learned, in our charitable work, how much truth there is in this terrible cry. It is to such girls that the doors of families of moderate means and medium position could open and admit them to a happy refuge. And my earnest advice to girls who are not able to earn a respectable support in stores, and also to those who find the confinement injurious to health, is to learn housework, and make themselves invaluable in the family of some good woman who needs just such assistance."

"There's another wrong thing ladies do," said the Sprightly Lady, "and while we are arraigning the poor things, we might just as well mention everything. They often engage two or three servants for the same place, thinking that if the first fails to keep her engagement, the next may come."

"Yes," replied Mrs. Hughes; "I once knew a woman who considered herself a Christian lady, who did such a thing. She said that the unreliability of the servants had driven her to it, and that she was obliged to protect herself. I confess I am unable to understand the peculiar construction of the intellect of any such woman; and as for her conscience, it —"

"Must be made of old shoe-leather," said the Sprightly Lady.

"Mrs. Hughes, what do you think of a lady searching a servant's trunk?" asked Dolly.

"Let me ask a question," was Mrs. Hughes's answer. "What do you think of a servant searching a lady's trunk?"

"Fortunately," observed the Millionnaire, with

a satisfied smile, "we are not called upon to consider such a monstrosity."

"I think you are mistaken," said Mrs. Hughes, in those chillingly polite tones that made me look about me for my spring overcoat. "I once knew of a servant doing just such a thing. She was dismissed, and on packing her trunk she missed a nightgown, and later one of the family found her looking through her mistress's closets and bureau-drawers for it."

"What an outrage!" murmured the Imitation Millionnaire.

"So the family thought, though there was no pretence about the girl's loss; she had really missed the gown, for several weeks later the next servant found it somewhere in the room. Her mistress loudly condemned her impudence; and yet that very woman had again and again searched the trunks and drawers of her servants when they were out."

"Oh, that's quite a different thing!" said the Millionnaire.

"Yes; but different only as regards the persons who do it," said Mrs. Hughes. "The two acts are one in their injustice and wrong. The trunk of a servant and her personal wardrobe are as strictly private property as anything her mistress can possess, and to intrude upon her privacy without her knowledge or permission is an outrage against justice and right."

"Pray, Mrs. Hughes, what is a lady to do if she misses articles and suspects her servants?" asked the Imitation Millionnaire.

"As far as I am concerned, I should be very slow to suspect a servant. Her character is her all, and I should feel very tenderly toward it. I have several times known articles in my house to be missing for a long time,—once it was almost a year, and I had made such search that I could have taken an oath in court that they were not upon the premises,—and yet, after all, they turned up in some most unexpected place. Twice, the circumstantial evidence was very strong against some servant I had at the time. But when the articles were found, long after I had ceased to look for them, I assure you I was more than thankful that never, by word or look, had I intimated to these servants a suspicion of their honesty. One should have, I think, many and excellent proofs before impeaching the character of a servant. But if a lady has reasonable cause to believe a girl dishonest, and thinks she would be likely to find stolen goods about her, then she should send for the proper officer to make a search. If I were the lady, I should still attempt to spare and save the girl. I should not let the officer see her until I had talked with her. I should tell her he had come, and that if she was unwilling to let me make the search, I should call him to do it. In most cases the girl would be terrified at the thought of an officer's presence, and would greatly prefer to have her mistress make the search. If I found nothing suspicious, I should dismiss the man without letting him see the girl. I think I should do that anyhow, unless the case was a very aggravated one; for the very pity I showed in this respect, and my desire to shield her from shame, might help me to save her."

"What else that's naughty do mistresses do?" asked the Sprightly Lady. "Give it to 'em! give it to 'em! I thirst for a recital of iniquities."

"I am afraid I cannot gratify you further to-day; not for lack of material, but because I am just now occupied with my own sin of having detained you all again."

With this the meeting adjourned, and I sought Dolly at once to question her, assuring her that I would shut her up in the back parlor if I learned that she had ever done any of those very reprehensible things I had heard discussed.

CHAPTER XI.

BRAINS IN HOUSEKEEPING.

UPON the next assemblage of the Club, Mrs. Hughes's face wore an expressive smile, the meaning of which she soon explained.

"I have been wondering this morning," she said, "if we do not want our servants to be perfect."

"Not I!" exclaimed the Sprightly Lady. "I don't want anybody in the kitchen so much better than poor Billy and I."

"No," said the Practical Person, more quietly, "I don't think we want them to be perfect."

Then the smile on Mrs. Hughes's face broadened, and became still more expressive.

"It would be interesting, then," she said, "to decide upon the faults we prefer."

This observation caused a deep silence to fall upon the unusually animated Club; and as the silence seemed likely to remain otherwise unbroken, Mrs. Hughes continued her remarks.

"Let us choose uncleanliness," she said.

This brought down upon the speaker a storm of dissent.

"By no means!" exclaimed the Practical Person, when the chorus was stilled. "That is about the worst fault a servant can have. One can do nothing with a dirty girl."

"Well, then, let it be sloth," suggested Mrs. Hughes.

But no, that would not do; she would never accomplish her work. Better an ugly temper, a lack of system, a disposition to run out too much. Mrs. Hughes was accommodating, for when any particular fault would not do she immediately had another to offer; but one by one they were rejected, until even her long list was at an end. Then it was that the smile I had first noted assumed its broadest and most meaning aspect.

"Ladies," she said, "in future let us always be careful to choose perfect maids."

The Practical Person laughed.

"I will confess now," she said, "that I would like to, though at first I did n't think so. But I've no doubt that all the servants I ever get will have plenty of faults, and I shall not have much to do in choosing them."

"Now, that is just where I hope you will permit me to differ from you," exclaimed Mrs. Hughes, with more animation than usual.

"Some one was once asking me about the choice of a servant, and I spoke of some virtues for which I always looked. Now, I may add that I always deliberately make a choice of faults. I, too, would like perfect servants; but—"

"They don't grow," interrupted the Sprightly Lady.

"No," continued Mrs. Hughes; "and since they must have faults, I want to have some choice in these. For instance, I have found that a quick, energetic, systematic girl may make an excellent kitchen servant with proper management, even though she have a hot temper; but it is almost impossible for her to become a good nurse. The work of a nurse is necessarily subject to manifold interruptions and upheavals, and requires endless patience. Although a girl in this position is the better for some system, yet she cannot arrange her work as she could in the kitchen; and if she tries to do this, and go through it quickly and undeviatingly, she is sure to have her patience overwhelmed sooner or later."

"I have learned that," said Dolly. "I once had a cook who rarely ever had a meal on time. She was slow and unsystematic; but she was so faithful, respectable, and sensible, that I hated to give her up. I tried every way for four months,—pushing and arranging,—but nothing would do. At last I hit upon a happy thought. I persuaded her to go into my nursery; and she is there to-day,— one of the best nurses I ever had. She is never out of patience; and by slowly but steadily pursuing her way she accomplishes a great deal of sewing, besides caring faithfully for the children. She is more under my eye in the nursery, and by some management she has learned to be as systematic as her work will permit; about the children's hours of feeding, and so forth, she is very regular, and she has opportunity to rest her nature for this unnatural effort between times."

"My own experience causes me heartily to endorse the lesson taught by this instance," said Mrs. Hughes. "There are, of course, some faults which we would never choose and should never tolerate; but it is undoubtedly true that a trait of character which is a fault in one position becomes a virtue in another. Aside from this very delightful and unmanageable class of failings, there is another class which may at least be modified by their situation,— that is to say, some faults are more bearable, or less annoying, in one situation than in another; and if we think of all this when we are selecting a servant, we shall be more likely to find we have the right woman in the right place than if we are careless of such matters."

"Mrs. Hughes, don't you think that most of us would have to buy an extra supply of brains before we could do all you suggest?" asked the Sprightly Person.

"I have always tried to prove to unbelievers that housekeeping is brain-work, if properly conducted. Indeed, it is quite a scientific occupation."

"Please, ma'am, what is to become of those of us whose brains were omitted in our general make-up?" said the Sprightly Lady, drawing down her face.

"I think *you* have no need to ask that question," Mrs. Hughes replied, with a laugh. It was quite evident that she agreed with me in an admiration for the Sprightly Person. "There are, however, many women, as there are many men, unable to do justice to any occupation calling for much intellect; and if these people keep house they will have to do their best, but they can never reach the results that will reward the more intellectual worker. But it is my belief that the large majority of women could do far better in this work than they are now doing, and consequently enjoy far greater advantages. Take this servant question, which, in most families lies at the very root of success or failure in housekeeping. Let a woman use her brains, and if they are small cultivate them. Let her choose and adapt wisely, and the battle is half won."

"I think system has much to do with good housekeeping," said the Practical Person.

"It undoubtedly has. There are many people to-day who have the reputation of being devoted housewives and mothers, — women who are thought to have an immense amount of work on hand, and who are pitied for their severe labors and admired for their self-sacrifices, — who are very little more than unsystematic and ignorant persons."

"That sounds rather severe, Mrs. Hughes," said a Silent Member; and I made a mental note to the effect that this rather tight shoe was pinching the lady.

"It does, indeed," Mrs. Hughes replied; "but when you see one woman labor hard and spread over an entire day work that another accomplishes without much effort in a few hours, what else can you think?"

"You can scarcely compare the housework of any two women," said the Practical Person.

"Not exactly, to be sure; but you can do so to a certain extent. I know a lady who has seven children. She is an attentive wife and mother, and engages in many social pleasures in addition to keeping a house, and yet she finds much more time for reading than another lady whom I also know, who has but one child and boards."

"I wish I knew how to systematize my work," sighed a Silent Lady.

"One has to study to learn that," said Mrs. Hughes. "One secret is, I think, in the matter of choice. I have read that conversation is merely a fine selection, and system is largely composed of the same element. One cannot attend to everything. Housework should, like the business in a store, be divided into departments, and servants should be trained and required to take charge of certain of these, and be held responsible for their proper care."

"Children are what require the most time," said the Practical Person.

"Yes, and very properly; but children receive a great deal of unnecessary care, and lack much that is necessary. If we examined into the matter, I think we should find that the majority of mothers spend more time upon the clothing of their children than upon their minds."

"But our children must be clothed," urged the Practical Person.

"Yes," said the Sprightly Lady, "unless we remove to that pleasant clime in which I once read of a planter's small son who was decked for company in a straw hat and a cane."

"Yes, they must be clothed," said Mrs. Hughes. "But we have all learned that there are clothes and clothes. It was always my effort, in making my children's garments, to learn of the easiest possible styles that would be pretty; for I do not believe in mortifying a little one's flesh and spirit by homely clothing. Then I taught my children to be very careful of what they wore, and in this way to preserve their clothes a long time. That is a useful lesson for the character of a child, boy or girl, as well as useful for one's time."

"But I don't think you can expect children to sit still continually," said a Silent Member.

"Why, no; I am sure mine did not, but for their rough-and-tumble play they had very strong, plainly-made clothes, and these they changed for something prettier later in the day, when their most boisterous play was ended. Children can run about a great deal, be very lively, and have a good time, without injuring nice clothes. Of course, when it comes to climbing fences and trees and wrestling, they ought to wear something pretty strong."

"That, fortunately, does not apply to little girls," sighed the Imitation Millionnaire.

"It applied to my little girls," said Mrs. Hughes. "They were always allowed and encouraged to engage in active sports."

"Mrs. Hughes," said Dolly, "I wish you would please give us an outline of your day."

"Perhaps I had better give you an outline of my day a few years back, for I am a little farther along in my housekeeping experiences than most of you, and as a woman's children grow older she has to alter her plans. When I had but one baby I had a great deal of time. Our means then would not admit of much company. We entertained often, but not formally; our friends dropped in occasionally and were made at home. I had a nurse whom I trained carefully; and excepting the time required to superintend my housework, I had almost the entire day to myself, for Mr. Hughes did not come home to luncheon. I taught my nurse needlework, and she did all the sewing of the family, and all except the finest mending, which I did evenings while talking with my husband or listening as he read aloud. I had my own particular little room in which I painted; and then, as the smell of the paint is apt to be somewhat injurious, I studied and read in another room; but I was alone when I worked, and the servants did not disturb me unnecessarily."

"They must have had a good time, all alone through the day," said the Practical Person.

"They were not alone very long at a time," replied Mrs. Hughes, quietly. "My nurse sat in the nursery, and was near at hand, and every half-hour or so I used to step in there to see if all was well, and have a few minutes' romp with my baby.. Then I used to take occasional excursions through my little house, during the day, and as the servants never knew when I was coming, they had little chance to deceive me, even if they had been so inclined; but I never kept servants who would wilfully disobey or deceive me."

"That might work very well if the children were not sickly," said the Practical Person.

"You can prevent children from being sickly," said Dolly.

"Certainly," said Mrs. Hughes, "and should do so. Parents have no right to bring a sickly child into the world; and when a child is born healthy, he will continue so most of the time if he is properly fed and cared for. But all that belongs more strictly to the subject of children, and we must not encroach upon it in this Club. I only diverged a moment, to explain that my children were seldom away from my care for an hour, whether indoors or out. When they took their exercise, I had them kept near at hand, unless I sent the nurse off on an errand with them. I always knew where they were. When I had more than one child, and the oldest was between two and three, I began spending more time with them. Then my plan of work was something like this: I rose at half-past six in winter, and six in summer. Until half-past nine I saw to my household, looking over the stores, giving orders and directions for any extra duties, attending to my accounts, and in general running over my entire housework for the day. I am naturally slow, I think, but I forced myself to learn celerity, and I managed to despatch a great deal in that time. I gave my whole attention to it, and let nothing unnecessary distract me. At half-past nine I retired to my room and had an hour and a half of intellectual work. Then from eleven until one I was with my children, most of the time outdoors. At that period I often did my marketing. I never went far for this, for I did not think the pennies saved atoned for the time lost; and time has always been of great value in my eyes. When I was with my children I joined in their games, and talked to them as improvingly and interestingly as my own information would permit me to do. And I may here remark that I was led to study many of the natural sciences that I might have something of account to tell my children when we were together. At one o'clock they were put to bed for a two-hours' nap, and I lay down for an hour; then I had three hours to myself before I again took them. Sometimes the older one would have a book, and sit quietly with me for a while in the afternoon. At six we dined."

"Well," said the Sprightly Lady with a great sigh, "I am so thankful you have at last seated yourself to eat something! You must be almost starved!"

"Oh, no," said Mrs. Hughes, laughing. "I ate before six, but really our dinner was the only meal of the day that occupied much time. We have always dressed for dinner, and taken it very leisurely. Generally we finished it by drinking our coffee in the library. We frequently had a friend to dinner."

"This," said the Millionnaire, "is the first mention of a social nature we have heard. Did you never make or receive calls?"

"Very seldom; I lost but little time or strength for the visiting around in which so many women indulge. Most of our evenings were devoted to social pleasures, but neither my husband nor myself had much daylight to spare. I was talking awhile ago with a friend whose mind is decidedly intellectual, albeit the illness of her husband and herself has prevented her, until lately, from indulging her tastes. Just now there is nothing of that kind to claim her time, and as she has no children, and is living for the present with a married sister, she ought to be able to command much leisure. But unhappily the sister has two children, who have been trained indeed, but trained to require most of the time of those around them; and, still more unfortunately, she has a neighbor, who, as she told me, was in the habit of running in almost daily and sitting for two or three hours."

"*Setting*, I should call that!" said the Sprightly Lady.

Even Mrs. Hughes's elegance could not restrain her smile.

"Yes," she replied, "it has occurred to me at times, that for some women to say they were going in to *set* with a neighbor was not, after all, as ungrammatical as would at first appear. I am sure I cannot tell why women of a higher class and higher aims permit anything of the kind."

"Oh, well, Mrs. Hughes," said the Practical Person, "sometimes one's neighbors are kindly people, who like to run in and out freely, and one does not want to be disagreeable to them."

"It is a peculiar and unfortunate feature of social life in villages, towns, and even new or small cities, I believe, but I see no reason for encouraging it. I believe in kindness to everybody; but I think kindness has nothing to do with this matter, for I know of no good gained on either side by these gossiping hours, and certainly there is a loss of much time that should be valuable to both. If a neighbor were in any trouble and I could be of help, I would go, by all means, and stay as long as my home duties would possibly permit. Ever since I began my housekeeping in a tiny cottage, I have lived on pleasant terms with my neighbors, but we have never run back and forth. I think that possibly I may have been called odd by them."

"'A crank' is the favorite term," suggested Dolly.

"Well, even 'crank' would not have frightened me; but as I never gossiped with any one, I failed to learn what my neighbors thought of me, and there was never anything unpleasant in their greetings when I met them."

"But, Mrs. Hughes, everybody knew that you were an artist, and so they excused you from making calls," said a Silent Member.

"They would have had to excuse me even if I had no such occupation, for long ago I became convinced that the time spent in making and receiving calls was almost all wasted. In one of his essays, Emerson says that no call ought to exceed ten minutes except by special invitation; I would go a step farther, and abolish most of the calls now made in what is considered society. Who ever saw a lady who did not count the paying of calls a disagreeable duty, and who did not often hope the acquaintances she was apparently striving to meet would be away from home? Such a thing is hollow, false, and it ought to be abolished. Life is too short, too real, for such sham, and time too precious for such waste."

"I fear you are a social fiend, Mrs. Hughes; this strikes me as a new and alarming phase of socialism. I shall look out for a bomb under my chair the next time I go to your house," said the Sprightly One, holding up her hands in mock horror.

"I really think, Mrs. Hughes," said the Imitation Millionnaire, with a fashionable air of superiority, "that if these ideas were carried out they would abolish society."

"Possibly so," said Mrs. Hughes, "though I am not sure they are forcible enough to accomplish quite so much good. This is no place to enter into a prolonged discussion of social subjects, and I have already digressed. I was trying, however, to explain why I always found time for my own education and also that of my children, although I was a housekeeper. I saved not only time, but also money, by abstaining from society so called, and I put the extra money on my service, and it has repaid me tenfold."

"Well, Owen Meredith says one may live without love, so he has something to eat; but he expresses it a trifle differently, I believe," said the Sprightly One.

"Ah! but I did not live without love, even of a social kind," said Mrs. Hughes. "I had a few intimate lady friends with whom I sometimes walked when I took my children out, and then we rarely sat down to dinner alone; indeed, the stroke of six might be said to have sounded the tocsin for social delights. Some evenings Mr. Hughes and I kept for ourselves, and we read, studied, played, and talked together at home, or went out, as we felt inclined; but generally, with the exception of an hour I have always taken for reading after dinner, we spent the entire evening socially; and most delightful has this mode of life proved. Music, reading aloud, and conversation have made the hours all too short. One evening a week, as you know, we have taken for our reception-night, and a great many of our friends always come in then."

"But when do you return all those calls?" asked the Imitation Millionnaire.

"Never!" said the Sprightly Lady. "She hasn't been to my house in a year."

"No, I could never look upon a call as a debt to be paid. We call upon all our friends once in a while, but we cannot go to each house very often, as we have quite a large circle. But I never hesitate about going to a friend's because I happen to remember that I have been there several times since she came to see me. If I have the time and the wish, I go, without casting up accounts with her first. A large number of our friends are, and always have been, young ladies and gentlemen, and they keep no calling accounts with us."

"I should think there would be danger, however, Mrs. Hughes," said the Imitation Millionnaire, gravely, "that such a very independent course would cut you off from all invitations from the better, more fashionable class."

"It does from the fashionable, but not from the better class. Mr. Hughes and I rarely have an invitation to a large party or reception, and still more rarely go. But little dinners of six, eight, and ten people, invited to meet some interesting artist, actor, or lecturer, we often attend, and also give, now that our means permit us to do so. Indeed, we began giving little dinners of this kind years ago, when we were far from wealthy."

The Imitation Millionnaire bit her lip and said nothing; she knew she would be greatly flattered to be invited to some of the many dinners Mrs. Hughes had attended and given.

"Another form of social entertainment in which we have often indulged is a Musicale, and still another, a Reading. At both of these we often have a little dance, and always a charming time. But I feel that I must crave pardon again, for I have afflicted you with a long digression."

"We brought it on ourselves, Mrs. Hughes," said the Sprightly Lady, "and I think we can very comfortably endure the affliction. For my part, I want more; I wish you would tell us what you think of George Eliot's story, 'The Sad Fortunes of the Reverend Amos Barton.'"

"I can easily understand why you ask," said Mrs. Hughes, with a laugh, "but we must not continue this theme longer. At our next meeting, if the ladies are interested in hearing it, I will very willingly give you my opinion of that story."

CHAPTER XII.

A MOTHER'S RIGHTS AND DUTIES.

"NOW, Mrs. Hughes," said Dolly, upon the next assemblage of the Club, "let us hear about the sad Barton."

The rest of the ladies joined in this request, and one of the Silent Members said, —

"I am especially interested in this, for I can't imagine how that story can have any bearing on our last topic of discussion."

"I can," said the Sprightly Lady. "Come, Mrs. Hughes, take up Millie Barton; I know she'll get a good scoring."

"The bearing is simply this: Millie Barton has, I believe, by the great majority of her readers, been held up to admiration as a model wife and mother, — a very beautiful type of womanhood. I used to draw down such indignation on my head, in my younger days, by dissenting from this view, that I generally kept silent, unless the subject was forced upon me."

"You don't mean to say you don't admire Millie Barton?" gasped a Silent Member.

"I am afraid I do mean that," said Mrs. Hughes, gently. "I may seem unappreciative; but in my mind I find but little admiration for Millie Barton, and but little pity for Amos Barton. The story is beautiful, as far as wording and life-painting are concerned. As types, the characters are excellently drawn; but as objects of admiration and pity, I think they fail. You remember that the story opens with a picture of Millie Barton walking the floor with her baby, and glancing wistfully at a large pile of stockings which must be mended ere she retires. Now that sounds devoted and pathetic; but if we shed the light of common-sense and intellect upon it, I think the picture fades. It has always seemed to me that any woman who was found walking the floor with a healthy year-old baby at ten o'clock at night was simply a bad manager. My children were never walked to sleep, unless suffering from ear-ache or some other pain, which we took all possible means to soothe. Long before ten o'clock a baby should be asleep; and it will be, without trouble, if its mother shows any judgment and common-sense."

"But surely Millie Barton had great need to overwork, with her poverty and large family," said a Silent Member, whose face was seamed with cares.

"Yes," said Mrs. Hughes; "and if the large family were necessary we would pity her, and commend her for her patient cheerfulness. Long ago, when I was very young and inexperienced, I read that story; but although I was deeply affected then by its simple pathos, I yet felt that in some way it was keyed upon a false note. Some years later I re-read it very carefully, and then I saw more clearly than I had before been able to see, wherein the falsity lay. The hero is so unheroic, that he discovers scarcely a single commendable trait. Pitiably narrow and ignorant in his religious life; criminally ignorant in his domestic life; a man whose conceit and selfishness prevented him from seeing that his wife was dying by inches; a creature decidedly of the earth, too ignorant to know it was a sin to bring into the world human beings for whom he and his wife had not the means and strength to provide, — that man is faithfully pictured for us, but he is not held up to contempt; for we are constrained to feel that the author, in her heart, not only pities him but even cherishes toward him a tender feeling."

"Well, whatever George Eliot may think of Mr. Amos, she evidently holds Mrs. Amos up as a model," said the Sprightly One.

"Yes, she is represented as an ideal of lovely womanhood. But I confess she seems to me but little more than a beautiful, sweet-tempered animal. She displays very little intellect ; her love is of the unreasoning kind. She evidently has no knowledge of her own rights, and knows nothing of the right of a child not to be born unless the parents can furnish means of proper provision. She even slights the rights of her maid, for the first picture describes the overworked servant, who had been ironing all day, as taking the baby at ten o'clock at night to put him to sleep, because, perchance, his presence in the sitting-room may be an annoyance to his father. Such things are wrong ; and it is largely in order to enable us to prevent them that we are given an intelligence so superior to that with which the brutes are endowed. By her injudicious indulgence of that year-old baby, Millie Barton wronged him, her maid, herself, and her unborn child. Take another point ; the woman who could, after all the suffering she had undergone at the hands of his ignorance and selfishness, pronounce Amos Barton a *good* husband, was herself sadly lacking in those higher intellectual traits and in that spiritual insight which should distinguish the human from the merely animal."

"But don't you suppose, Mrs. Hughes, that this was a faithful picture of those times?" asked a Silent Member.

"Yes, and, alas! of these times also, in many households. I don't doubt that George Eliot in this, and some other instances, wrote according to her day and her nation; but a great writer should be far ahead of her day, and her nation too, for that matter, if need be. A writer should be a leader, and no leader should tarry in the present, but should dip into the future. Dickens presents the grossest wrongs in his works, but he does not label them *rights*. He paints them in such plain colors, that even one accustomed to a narrow sphere of thought and life cannot mistake his meaning, at least. I recently read, in the London 'Spectator,' an excellent remark. The writer said that the chief error of the tale he was reviewing consisted in its presentation of useless and purposeless self-sacrifice as something noble, heroic, and admirable. That brought to my mind this story of George Eliot. Surely there are enough opportunities in life for the display of real womanhood, without dragging in those occasions which should only rouse a noble indignation and refusal, and representing their endurance as womanly! Surely there are enough opportunities for true motherhood, without presenting under that head those that merely show that, like an affectionate animal, the woman loves without being able to see what is for the best good of her child. Real motherhood should always excite our strongest admiration; but we should be able to tell the fictitious from the true, the injudicious from the wise, and to detect sentimentality, even when it is labelled sentiment. Natural history tells of a gall-insect that sacrifices its own life in order to preserve the lives of its young. Immediately after laying its eggs it covers them with its body, and pins the edges of the latter to the ground all around, in such a manner as to protect the eggs but to cause its own death. This certainly is the highest type of motherly devotion in an insect, but in the human mother we look for something more. Her life should be of greatest value to her children, and should be preserved for their sake if not for her own. But Millie Barton, like that insect, so pinned her life down about her household, and so drained her vital powers, that her lamp of existence went out, and her little ones were left to be an unnatural burden upon their young sister, who herself needed the care and training of the mother whose life had been so needlessly and wrongly sacrificed."

"Well, Mrs. Hughes," said the member with the very careworn face, "it may be easy to convince us, but I think you would have to make men over."

"Not all of them: there are some truly manly men, even now; but if that were necessary, it is no impossible task. Indeed, any woman who has a son whom she is not making over, as you call it, is falling far short of true motherhood, and is doing the greatest wrong to some future woman. Another sentence, which I read in the book reviews of the same paper, is worthy of most serious attention. It occurs in an excellent article on a book called, 'The Problems of a Great City.' Speaking of the problem which arises from the fact that the criminal and idle will have children, the writer says: 'We have first to make the comfortable classes understand *morality* in this respect. Until we can make the healthy and impecunious curate, whose death would leave a wife and six children penniless, feel true shame at his position, it is useless to expect the criminal and idle classes to understand and act upon the law of population.' The suggestions embodied in this sentence are not only suitable for grave consideration, but they demand it, and it is wrong to try to put them aside. Another article in this same paper speaks of the masses on this globe, for which, as it says, after a comparatively short period, there will not be even breathing-space to be found. We have all heard people seriously speak of fires, cyclones, pestilences, and various other disasters, as God's means of diminishing the number of human beings. For years, now, the question, not only as regards professions and almost all occupations, but in Europe even respecting territory itself, has not been of population, but of over-population. This may seem to some of the Club a long and inexcusable digression, but I cannot conceive how a woman can realize the dignity of her position as housekeeper, and fulfil its duties properly, unless she have a proper conception of her dignity and her rights as wife and mother; and the latter necessarily and primarily involves just such questions as we have been discussing, taking that story as our text. The subject of time is closely interwoven with that of housekeeping, and upon this topic we hear many ignorant opinions from the lips of those who should utter wisdom. I know a young lady of intelligence and gifts, who recently made a visit to the home of a married brother. She told me that the question as to whether or not she ought to pursue her art (of painting) if she married, had often come up in her mind; but after her experiences with her brother's children, she saw that it would not be right to do so. I differ from her widely, feeling certain that she would commit an actual wrong were she to neglect this gift. In reading the Parables, I cannot discover that Christ made any exception in favor of women, when he forbade the hiding of a talent in a napkin."

"But what is to be done if a woman's household duties prevent her from exercising her talent?" asked the Practical Person.

"If she has assumed household cares, I should say their claim was the stronger of the two. There are cases where women possess a talent whose exercise would materially interfere with the proper performance of household duties, and possess it in such a marked degree that to me it seems plain God did not intend they should marry. I think there are men, too, who are set apart for a single life, by God's having given them some especial work which would interfere with their duties as husband and father. But my own experience, as well as the experience of many older and abler women, has shown me that it is only a vocation of an exceptional kind which must of necessity prevent, for man or woman, the proper performance of the duties belonging to married life."

"Mrs. Hughes, did you think about this before you were married?" asked Dolly.

"Yes; I was led to think of it. I was instructed and taught by wise parents to look about me observingly and intelligently. The men or women who postpone such study until after marriage are sure to bring a great deal of trouble upon themselves, and on others who are innocent of the mistake or wrong. Ever since I was a very young girl my mind has been busily revolving the problems of woman's life and work. I have travelled some, visited some, been in a number of households, and even as a girl it was my custom to study the workings of those households. In most of them I must say that I regarded much that I saw as one regards a warning sign-board. 'Go and do *not* likewise,' was the command I frequently seemed to hear; but there were homes in which I saw such good management, such an admirable union of heart and brain, that I was fain to sit at the feet of the mistress and learn of her. And so when I took charge of a home of my own, my mind was well stored with theories, the result of observation and thought. Among other aims these stood out prominently,— the establishment of an attractive and comfortable home with the least expenditure of money; the proper care of infants with the least expenditure of time and strength; and the development of the character of my servants. At first came the struggle which is the almost inevitable attendant upon an adjustment of theory to practice. I do not claim that the work is ended, nor that it ever will be ended; there will always be need for study, thought, and endeavor to exercise the highest powers. But I have year by year been finding my task less difficult, and I believe that it will continually grow so."

"Don't you think, Mrs. Hughes, that women have many wrongs inflicted on them?" asked a Silent Member, whose face told its story.

"I sometimes think that women are the most deeply wronged of all God's creation; but on looking about me I am bound to confess that in most cases they themselves are mainly responsible for these wrongs. Such ignorance of their rights; such failure to show common-sense, reason, judgment,— to put their brains into the care of their households and children, — as one sees on every side, is fairly disheartening. And worse still, not only are women guilty of these grave errors, but there is a false note running through their creed, and on that note is keyed the cry that these same errors are virtues; that these and not their opposite mean womanliness, true wifehood, and motherhood. Never was a falser note sounded!"

"You do think, then, that women are inferior to men, Mrs. Hughes!" exclaimed the Frivolous Person; and she seemed rather delighted.

"By no means," answered Mrs. Hughes, with unusual force. "In looking closely into the affairs of men, one can discern much of the same stupidity and ignorance, modified necessarily by a man's being out in the world more and gaining some sense by hard knocks. But however that may be, it is over my own sex that I chiefly mourn, because their work is the more important of the two, and hence their errors are more disastrous than the errors of men. In my more sanguine moments I hope that an entirely different state of affairs will be brought about, and in my most sanguine I firmly believe it will. At present, I venture to assert that there is not one woman out of a hundred whose household management would betray that admirable union of heart and brains which should form the true womanly ideal. When women become women indeed, we shall have educated mothers educating their children. Public schools will then be relegated to their proper place, and become the foster home of the lower classes chiefly, — those whose parents are prevented by ignorance or the needs of toil, or probably by both, from educating them; and then perhaps these schools will not continue to teach French, Latin, Greek, and some other branches, at the public expense."

"You believe, then, in limiting the small low-born boy's knowledge?" said the Sprightly Lady.

"No; but I believe in letting him work for his education beyond a certain point. But this subject has not even as much excuse for claiming our consideration as the last, and I must forego it. Indeed, I feel I must for the hundredth time ask pardon for digression, and again promise better conduct in the future."

CHAPTER XIII.

METHODS OF HOME GOVERNMENT.

UPON the next assemblage of the Club, I observed that the Frivolous Young Person was missing. "I knew it!" I exclaimed mentally; "I knew she could n't stand that last meeting!" I always was able to foretell anything after it occurred. A few of the other ladies seemed to have had their enthusiasm a trifle dampened, owing, I suppose, to the fact that they had talked the last meeting over with their husbands. But Mrs. Hughes was not a woman to be moved by anything of that kind. She was too just and too calm to allow any opposition to cause her to waver from an action or a word she deemed right. At the same time she was far from being a contentious woman, or one who lacked wisdom enough to see when it was time to be silent. And having said all she thought necessary to say for a time on those vital questions, she brought forward other subjects. Her control over those with whom she associated was, to casual observers, wonderful; but the secret lay, not alone in her mental power, but also in her gentle courtesy, her justice, and her tender, sympathetic nature.

"We were speaking," she said, on opening the meeting,—for she had long since acceded to the wish of the Club that she should be its leader,— "several meetings ago, I think it was, we were speaking of the matter of engaging servants, and their asking many questions at that time. It seems to me that the best plan is for the mistress to volunteer answers to these questions before they are asked, if we may so express it. The latter is my plan. After asking a girl about various things, I say: 'Now I suppose that you want to know all you can about the place I have to offer you.' And then I tell her, not only what wages I will give, but also of what my family consists, and what her work and her privileges will probably be. I am very minute, both for her sake and also for my own, for I find that all is apt to run more smoothly when there has in the first place been a perfect understanding."

"Mrs. Hughes," said Dolly, "will you please tell me something about governing servants."

"As much as I can; but it is difficult to condense that subject into a few words. There are, or should be, various ways, for, as we said before, no two can be treated alike; and the successful mistress, like the successful mother or teacher, or any leader or governor, in fact, must be a student of human nature. But there are some general rules which, as far as my experience and study go, seem, with few exceptions, to be of value. One of these, for me at least, grew out of a hint I received from an article on a child's telling lies. The advice here given was to go out of one's way, if necessary, to convince the child that he lost whenever he told a falsehood, not by whipping him, — that was not recommended, — but by letting him find out that not only the advantage he strove to gain was lost, but some other advantage as well. This same rule can be applied to service, I think. For instance, if a girl is careless, I take great pains, generally without saying anything to her, to let her see that her carelessness costs her trouble. I have hanging in my kitchen a blank-book and pencil, so that the cook may set down any article needed from the grocery or butcher-shop. If she forgets to do this I let the omission pass, if possible, without notice, until some time when it is particularly inconvenient to her to go out after whatever article has been omitted from the order, and then I send her for it. Sometimes I speak of these things, by directing a careless girl's attention to the many needless steps she takes because she does not use her memory. I always try to see that the penalty for the carelessness or wrong-doing of a servant never falls upon any one but herself. This requires attention and management, of course. On the other hand, I show my servants that they gain by good service. Praise has always been with me a powerful instrument of government. I have rarely ever talked with a servant reprovingly, when I have not taken pains at the same time to notice something she did well, or some good trait she possessed. And I never fail to notice any attention or kindness, however slight, which my servants may show me. This always stimulates them to greater efforts to please. It is sometimes necessary to awe one's servants a trifle. For illustration, permit me to speak of a nurse I once had, but could only keep until I was able to supply her place, because of her temper. She never gave way to passion before me, but I knew that even her repressed irritability found a certain expression, and had a certain bad influence over the children. She belonged to a class with whom I dislike to deal, although I can if necessary. I had to keep her in order by demonstration of superior force and will-power. She never dared show anger to me, but I knew that she vented her ill-humors in my kitchen, — knew it because I knew that such a nature as hers must find an outlet, and because I noticed in the atmosphere of my house the effect of her angry complaints. But it astonished my cook very much when I told her one day that although I had not overheard a syllable that had been spoken, I knew what Charlotte was saying in the kitchen. Several times my knowledge of human nature, and of the inevitable consequences of certain conditions and elements of character, has impressed my servants with an idea that my oversight was not confined to the times of my presence."

"What do you do when a girl is impudent, Mrs. Hughes?" asked the Sprightly Lady.

"I never had an impudent servant."

"You must have been wonderfully fortunate in their dispositions, then," observed the Practical Person.

"No, I think not. This nurse, of whom I have been speaking, was a most high-tempered, proud-spirited girl. But although I had to talk to her sometimes in the plainest and even severest way, I never had an impudent word from her. She was a girl who could not keep any place, because of her temper. I only kept her two months, and would have parted with her sooner, but for the fact that I was ill and could not choose another girl. I felt sorry for her; she had had much to embitter her life. But although I did not feel it right to continue my children in her care, she knew that I understood and to a certain extent sympathized with her; knew, too, that when I reproved her I always had justice on my side; and I think that this same justice had even more control over her than my will. I always showed her, as I always show all my servants, that I am perfectly fearless. I show them, too, that I rely on their doing what is right by me. Once, when I was sick in bed, Charlotte went out for the afternoon without permission. It was the day which I usually gave her, but she knew that when I was ill she ought to consult me. I only discovered her absence by learning that my cook was unable to perform some service for my nurse because she had the children in charge. I said to my husband that I would talk to Charlotte and see that that never happened again. He advised me not to do so, as I would be in a great strait if she left at that time; but I had no fear, and on her return I summoned her to my room. I asked her very quietly how she came to go out without permission. She replied that it was her regular day. I said, 'I have never had a day when my servants are free to go out, come wind or rain or hail. You knew I was ill, and you should have asked if you could be spared.' She said she did ask Maggie, the cook, and she told her she could go. I almost smile now, when I think of how I drew myself up in bed, and spoke with such dignity, 'Charlotte, you will have to understand, once for all, that Maggie is not the one to give permission; as long as I live, I shall be mistress here.' At another time in my life I had an Irish cook who had been considerably petted and flattered. She had been receiving five dollars a week, and in addition to a very exalted opinion of herself, she possessed an ugly temper. There were many occasions during the time she lived with me, when nothing but the most careful management kept her from impudence. At the risk of being tedious, I will relate a scene that once took place between us. I have always insisted on having the servants air their room thoroughly, and one morning, on going into Bridget's room, I found that the window had not been opened. It was frozen down; but, as I had shown her before, a little hot water from the bath-room near by would suffice to thaw it. I went to work upon it this time myself, and just then she came upstairs. She felt, as I intended she should, tacitly reproved, and was angry. She began making up her bed, and I said, 'Bridget, the room is not aired, so you need not make the bed yet.' She muttered something about the bed not needing any more airing, and continued making it up. Again I said very quietly, as I worked away at the window, 'Bridget, I do not wish to have you make that bed now.' She proceeded to mutter and growl to herself, as she did when angry. It was a peculiar sound like distant thunder, and I always knew it threatened a storm, and was wary. She continued to make up the bed, and I said no more, but pursued my work, resolved to dismiss her if she really disobeyed me. But after she had half made it she left the room and went downstairs, still growling ominously. That day and the next I avoided my kitchen as a mariner avoids an ugly rock. When necessary to give directions, I did so as gravely and briefly as possible. I could see that Bridget's smothered rage gradually cooled, and on the third day she was all complaisance, — evidently anxious to make amends. Then she was in just the proper condition; and as her day's work had not been hard enough to fatigue her especially, that evening I summoned her to my room. I had her then in my power, so to speak, for her passion had passed away and left her defenceless. I gave her one of the plainest talks she ever had. I spoke kindly, and, as was my custom, showed I appreciated her good traits; yet I told her she had narrowly escaped dismissal, which would have been a great disgrace to her. I showed her how impossible it would be for me to maintain my position as mistress if I allowed any such conduct; and I told her that a repetition of the offence would of necessity part us. The woman had the good sense to see that justice was on my side, and she apologized for what she had done, and I never afterward had the same trouble with her, although I often left my kitchen because I knew that if I continued there I should be forced to notice some misdemeanor, reproof for which she was then in no mood to brook. That is, I think, the great secret of avoiding impudence on the part of servants; always be cool yourself, particularly with a hot-tempered girl, and if you have occasion for serious reproof, or if it is necessary to talk over a number of matters, select some time when she is not fatigued, when she is quiet and disposed to listen. And of all things, take her alone. Never make the mistake of reproving a servant before others; you mortify her, and the resentment she feels because of this humiliation almost invariably finds its outlet in impudence."

"I don't think they all are as sensitive as you suppose, Mrs. Hughes," said the Practical Person.

"I can only say," answered Mrs. Hughes, "that I should have no hopes of making anything out of a servant who was not somewhat stung and humiliated when reproved before others. Even in small matters I think it is very unwise to make any correction whatever before other persons. Indeed, it has always been my custom to do as much of my speaking as possible — directions and all — when I am alone with my servants. I find that this course tends to make them more quiet and respectful in their behavior about the house. I remember once visiting in a family where scarcely a meal passed without some conversation of this kind between the mistress and the maid. The mistress would perhaps discover that her plate was cold, and turn at once to the waitress: 'These plates are cold again to-day; I told you to look after this, and see that they were always warm.' And then the waitress would try to vindicate herself by saying, perhaps, 'I heated them myself to-day; they must have cooled.' And the mistress would further remark, 'They certainly have. I can't bear cold plates; it just spoils my dinner.' All this was very irritating to the servant and offensive to the listeners. Even if the lady had spoken to the girl alone, she should first have asked her to explain herself. Indeed, a mistress should always do that, for often there are circumstances connected with a fault that will partially if not wholly excuse it, and all this should be known before reproof is attempted. Some women seem deliberately to adopt a method which is admirably contrived in every way to make even a respectful girl impudent. I have heard mistresses of this kind nag their servants until they were exasperated, nettled, and stung into impertinence. Such a thing as calling reproofs up or down stairs, or even giving ordinary directions from one room to another, is not only unladylike but also unwise; and the result of such conduct is almost always a familiar if not impertinent manner on the part of the servant. This nagging is an especially irritating habit. I think that many faults should go unreproved. I once heard blindness earnestly recommended to teachers; and I think that in the same sense it might well be urged upon mistresses. But when it is necessary to reprove or direct, then do so, but make the remarks pithy and brief. Say what you have to in order to be clearly understood, and be done with it; repetitions weaken authority. Time, place, and manner all have to be consulted in dealing with servants, as with children. If a lady goes into her kitchen when the girl is just struggling with a large wash, or has just completed it, and takes her to task for some fault, she deliberately courts impertinence."

"'She woos, and should win,'" observed the Sprightly Lady.

"I certainly think so," said Mrs. Hughes. "Then, again, if she chooses a time when she herself is tired or excited, she must not expect good results. A lady should send for her servant, when it becomes necessary to reprove her seriously, and speak with her quite alone. Two things I have always made clear to my girls when I was reproving them, — one, that I had far rather bestow praise than blame, that I was really unhappy when matters went wrong and the good feeling between us was even temporarily impaired; and the other, that I tried in every way to do what was right and kind by them, to allow them every privilege possible, and in all ways to make their lives with me as pleasant as I could. I always appealed to them to know if this were not so, and then appealed to their sense of justice to know if I had not a right to look to them to do all in their power to make matters comfortable and pleasant for me. It would be a very strange girl who would be impudent if she were always dealt with in this way. I have never known such an one, and, as I said before, I have had some very high-tempered servants. I have had, too, even with my good servants, some occasions for discipline that might naturally have taxed their patience. I once had a very faithful girl, who, though quiet, was fond of going out. On one occasion I gave her permission to attend several entertainments that followed in close succession, on condition that she would be home at a certain time, —

eleven, I think. She overstayed the hour each night, always having an excuse, it is true. Saturday night came, and she asked if she could go to a sociable. I consented, only on condition that she should be home at half-past ten, setting an earlier hour because she had been so often delinquent. She did not come until half-past twelve. I had no doubt of the girl's good character, but I felt that, as its protector, I must take some decided measures. Sunday was her day out; but I summoned her to my room, talked with her, and told her finally that because she had abused my favors, she must not go out for a week. I know this was very hard for her, but she felt herself in the wrong, and she bore the penalty. After that I had no more trouble."

"Mrs. Hughes," said a Silent Member, "you spoke of being brief with servants. You don't believe, then, in talking with them very much?"

"Why, yes, I think I do, but only at the proper time and in the proper way. I have always conversed more or less with my servants, especially with my nurse. The latter is near me much of the time, and I am anxious to have her know my views, so as to be able to take care of my children intelligently. When I was a younger housekeeper, I had for three years a very valuable nurse, who came to me first as cook. I always recall with delight the remark made by an intimate friend after this girl had been with me for over a year. She said, 'Martha has changed very much since she first came to you. Her whole appearance is different. She shows in every way an improvement in character.' I earnestly hope that no girl ever lived with me as nurse any length of time without being, when she left, better prepared to take charge of a house of her own and bring up children, if she ever had any. I always endeavor to take such an interest in my servants that they will freely tell me where they have been when they go out. They almost always tell where they are going, and afterward I always ask if they had a pleasant time, and what went on; and I hope that this friendly interest protects them, as well as influences them favorably."

"I suppose, Mrs. Hughes, you don't approve of anything like familiarity with servants," said a Silent Member.

"Not under any circumstances. As I have often said, familiarity between mistress and maid is both undignified and improper; but there is a certain pleasant jesting way of treating servants, which, from some people toward some people, is very successful, and does not beget familiarity."

"Yes," said Dolly, "I know a lady who almost always governs her servants in that way. She is from the South, and has been accustomed to negroes all her life, and she has a certain manner that works wonders with those whom she undertakes to govern. Sometimes she is humorous, sometimes a trifle sarcastic, and sometimes she indulges in a little anger, which is about half real and half pretended, and then they all know she is not to be trifled with, and they fly around and do what she wants without delay. She is really a fascinating study to me; for with all this jocularity and ease of manner, she never loses her dignity, and I know that her servants would not dream of taking a liberty with her; sometimes they even stand a little in awe of her. But they are devoted to her and her interest; she can do almost anything with them. She says, though, that up North she finds a great difference in the servants. Many of them cannot be treated in that way. Indeed, she has had a few to whom she scarcely dare say Good-morning, for fear of their taking advantage of her, and straightway trying to be familiar. But I know that she does not feel at all at home with servants of that type, and she generally manages to have another kind about her."

"How does she talk to them?" asked a Silent Member.

"Oh, that is very hard to tell. If I were to

try to imitate I should probably only succeed in caricaturing her. I remember two or three little things I overheard her say, but I am afraid they will sound very flat repeated without her voice and manner. Once she had found the servants' room in great disorder, and she accosted her housemaid with, 'See here, Jane, I've just been up into your room, and I am mortified to think I have any girls in my house who would keep such a place. Even your hats were on the floor. If you go on this way, some day those hats will be missing, and you and Katie will have to go to prayer-meeting bareheaded.' One Sunday her nurse was out, and one of the other servants had charge of the children. For some reason she wished to have them bathed in a foot-tub instead of in the bath-room, but the foot-tub was missing. She told Jane, the housemaid, to look it up, saying that Bridget, the nurse, used it for the children the day before. I believe servants are notoriously poor searchers, and Jane proved no exception; for she appeared and said quietly and resignedly, 'The tub isn't to be found, ma'am.' My friend turned upon her, and with one of her inimitable expressions, half humorous and half severe, said, 'Of course you can't find it when it's not in the house. I suppose Bridget took it to Mass with her.' The girl's face broke into a smile as this ludicrous picture presented itself, and she hastily withdrew and — found the tub. Sometimes when her servants ask permission to go out in the evening, she'll say, 'Well, is it one or two o'clock to-night?' Then they say what time they'll be at home, and although she's very indulgent, she generally holds them to it. She gives the servants a vacation once in a while. Indeed, I think she watches very closely without saying much, and if she sees signs of fatigue she cries a halt, so to speak, in the work. During some of their vacations she pays their wages right on. Once, after she had been away herself, I heard her say to her cook, 'Well, Katie, I suppose you're crazy to be travelling now. You'll have to leave next.' Then the girl modestly told of a little visit she would like to make, and my friend at once arranged matters so that she could go. I don't know of any one who deals with servants more successfully than this lady, but her methods are inimitable."

"Yes," said Mrs. Hughes, "I know of another lady who has just such ways, and she, too, is from the South. I myself should never undertake any such style of government, for those manners and ways are not natural to me by birth or education, and if I attempted them I should fail to be fascinating and simply be coarse and familiar. I know a lady who attempts such ways and fails miserably. She herself is a Northerner, but her husband is from Kentucky, and she has probably learned something of this manner of governing servants from him. I have heard her go to the foot of the stairs and call to her housemaid, 'Sarah, here's a letter from your beau.' Her servants are almost always familiar with her, and often impudent, and she wonders why it is; but we can easily understand. The trouble is not in her words alone. When she tries to adopt this free-and-easy way, there is a certain indescribable something in tone and manner which marks the difference between the real and the imitation. The former is very successful with some servants, the latter is a great failure. But enough for to-day; we must be turning homeward."

"Ay!" said the Sprightly Lady, "'our noble husbands do lack us.'"

CHAPTER XIV.

CARE FOR SERVANTS' CHARACTER.

"MRS. HUGHES," said the Practical Person, when the Club next assembled, "some reference has been made to giving vacations to servants. Do you believe in that?"

"Yes; I give a yearly vacation of four weeks to all my servants, and pay their wages just the same. When I kept but one girl, she always found a substitute for me; but since I have kept more, I have generally so lessened and divided the work among the others that one could be spared. I know how tired girls become after working a long time, and I have found that these vacations are of great benefit. We ourselves need to break ranks once in a while, and our lives are less monotonous and our work generally more pleasant than theirs."

"I notice, Mrs. Hughes, that you often quote what your servants think about things," said Dolly. "I believe that one secret of your success with them is that you look at matters from their standpoint."

"I try to, for I think that, without this, justice would be an impossibility. Whenever I talk with them, either for reproof or in a friendly way, I encourage them to say what they think, so long as they do it respectfully. In this way I have learned much about the ordering of my work and managing my workers. Every now and then we hear of some large establishment, like John Wanamaker's in Philadelphia, and Pillsbury's Mills in Minneapolis, where a system of copartnership is in vogue, and the result of such a method has always, I believe, been satisfactory. I have tried something of that kind with my servants almost ever since I went to housekeeping, and it has worked well."

"What do you do?" asked the Imitation Millionnaire.

I noticed she did not speak as often as formerly, nor with as great confidence.

"I have only so far tried it with my cook, but I hope to find a way of carrying out the same plan with all my servants. I know just about what my butcher and grocer bill ought to be if ordinary care is taken to prevent waste. In the early days of our housekeeping twenty dollars was the figure for groceries, each month, and five dollars for meat. If the bills did not exceed this limit, the cook received an extra half-dollar on the first week of the succeeding month.

If the groceries came to any figure between eighteen and nineteen dollars, and the butcher's bill to four, the cook's premium was seventy-five cents, and so on."

"What did you do if the bills were over large?"

"I looked after matters more closely, and if the girl persisted in extravagance I dismissed her. But usually this plan resulted in more economy than any vigilance of mine in overlooking would have done, and saved me time and annoyance as well as money. Another point gained by making servants feel that they are in a manner partners in your establishment, is their own increase of dignity and self-respect. This is something I have always labored for; I try to make my girls sensitive to the disgrace of unfaithful, slack service. I continually impress them with the dishonesty of taking money for which they have but half worked, and the dignity of feeling that what they receive belongs to them by right of good labor. This self-respect and dignity of character I try in every way to inculcate, for it is a great safeguard. It enters into a servant's treatment of her male friends; into her sensitiveness about reproof, making her feel it a disgrace if she has to be watched like a child, for fear of forgetfulness, or punished in any way. The development of the character of our servants is a serious responsibility, — one from which no thoughtlessness on our part can free us. We are constantly hearing of railway reading-rooms, working-men's reading-rooms, and so on. How many mistresses provide reading for their servants?"

"It would be very hard, Mrs. Hughes, to know what kind to offer them," said the Practical Person.

"Yes, that is true; but one can find something. As a rule, they are interested in a class of reading suitable to children of average brightness, — children from seven to ten years old; although some servants are beyond this mark, and some have not yet reached it. Another point to be considered when we are thinking, as we always should, of our servants' characters, is care about the conversation overheard. I always shrink when any one in my house indulges in talk about lovers, and pressing hands, and all such silly nonsense, before my servants; for to them, with their crude ideas, and their knowledge of much moral laxity, all that has a worse sound than to us. And if they fancy such things are endorsed by those whom they are accustomed to regard as above them, the effect is bad. In the same way many foolishly indulge in jests on the subject of religion, or falsehood, or honesty, or some other virtue; and although they themselves may be quite correct in life, their influence on any who hear them must be bad, if they happen to be of a different or an ignorant class. Still another point to which we should look, when considering this subject of our servant's character, is extravagance. For their sakes, as well as our own, we should endeavor to make economy dignified and worthy of respect, and extravagance disreputable. Some people affect extravagance, or really indulge in it, thinking that it gives them an aristocratic air, — an air of having been accustomed to luxury. If they did but know it, such folly makes them contemptible in the eyes of all right-minded people, and gives them a dishonorable rather than an aristocratic air. You will almost always find that people who affect these ways have disgraceful unpaid bills in the background ; you will find that they think lightly of their credit, and that others do the same. To be forced into debt because of unexpected and unusual expenses is a great misfortune, but no disgrace; to be thrown into debt by reason of mismanagement is still more unfortunate, but no disgrace if the parties are doing their utmost to retrieve their errors and pay what they owe; but to deliberately make debts, and then go on living extravagantly while these are unpaid, and still worse, to make a display of such extravagance, is disreputable, and should, and does, sooner or later, blast the character of those who are guilty of such conduct."

Just at this point the Imitation Millionnaire became very busy arranging some of her draperies, and affected not to hear what was said.

"But, Mrs. Hughes," objected a Silent Member, "you spoke of teaching economy to our servants; setting them an example, I suppose you mean. But I don't quite see how we can do that; you surely would not have us live as it would be proper for them to live."

"Certainly not; but the different styles of living suitable for different people could, I think, easily be made clear to sensible girls. It seems to me that any one could appreciate the fact that Mrs. Jones, who is worth a million, has a right to dress more elegantly than Mrs. Smith, who is not worth a hundred. But the point that I would especially enforce is, that although some things that would be extravagant for Mrs. Smith are perfectly proper for Mrs. Jones, yet actual waste would be as sinful in one case as in another. We are doing a good work whenever we make economy — not parsimony, but economy — dignified and extravagance disgraceful. I once knew a young couple who, owing to the wicked indulgences of the man, became involved in debt, and were forced to break up housekeeping. The wife was young and very ignorant; and while in the main I doubt not she was desirous of doing right, yet I could not avoid seeing that, partly because of an unfortunate early training, and still more because of an association with her corrupt and dishonorable husband, her sense of honor was blunted. Although she and he had small butcher and grocer bills which they were unable to pay then, and had no prospect of ever paying, — bills which they felt they must ever allow to go unpaid, — yet she would talk to me of her husband's nice tastes; of how he would never use — what my entire family then used — castile soap, but must have a fine article. Disgust was the only emotion that this and more talk of the same nature inspired in me. We should have the same feeling, I think, toward those housekeepers who permit and even encourage extravagance in their kitchens. It is thought by some poor silly women to sound stylish to speak of the extravagance of an Irish cook. We Americans would do well to sit at the feet of the French for a few years and learn how to turn every bit and scrap into a dainty dish. That were an art to be proud of, indeed! And if we ourselves first learn and then teach such arts in our household, we can have the satisfaction of knowing that we are preparing our servants in that respect to make good homes of their own when the time comes."

"You were speaking a few moments ago, Mrs. Hughes," said Dolly, "about the best method of dealing with a child if he should tell stories. Do you think that one can reform an untruthful servant?"

"Why, yes," Mrs. Hughes answered with a smile; "otherwise I could not believe in future salvation. I certainly think that with God's help we may so strengthen and prop up weakness as to reform erring servants; it is somewhat more difficult to deal with viciousness, though I cannot believe that even that is beyond help. For our children's sake we must, however, forego doing much that would otherwise be our duty as well as pleasure. But as to this matter of truthfulness, I have known many cases where servants as well as children were terrified into falsehood. If a mistress is quick and severe, and her maid at all timid, in nine cases out of ten the latter will learn to tell lies to shield herself. We should be very careful not to frighten a weak or a gentle nature into this sin."

"I would like to ask about another point, Mrs. Hughes," said the Practical Person. "You spoke once, I think, of improving a slow girl. Is there any way of making such an one fast?"

"Perhaps not that, but I have seen such a servant improve greatly. Sloth is sometimes inborn, and expresses itself in the movements; but more frequently, I think, it is the result of a lack of system. I once had a servant whose slowness had its origin in both causes. I talked with her, appealing to her good sense and reason, as I always do. I told her that I knew she would like to make me feel happy about the work and her service; told her that her own life would be much easier and happier if she would form different habits; that as she was now she must either violate her conscience and perform her duties in a half-way manner, or else she must be oppressed by a knowledge of the existence of much work still undone. In the course of the talk I said that I used to be very slow myself, but that, as she already knew, I was now able to do some of her work in half the time that she required; and I suggested that she remedy her fault in the same way that I had remedied mine,— by giving herself a certain time in which to accomplish any particular piece of work, watching the clock and pressing forward to achieve this end. I advised her to force herself to be steadfast; to turn neither to the right nor to the left, either to talk with any one or look about her, but to learn to work while she worked, not at high-pressure rate, so as to cause great fatigue, but steadily and with reasonable celerity. Her lack of system I took in hand, arranging her work for her until she gradually learned to do this herself; and as she adopted my suggestions and tried hard to please me, she soon became, not a very rapid worker, but one who accomplished considerable, and was indeed a valuable servant."

"Mrs. Hughes, you were speaking of the moral effect a mistress might have upon her servants' character," said Dolly. "Do you ever try to impress any religious truths upon them?"

"This is a difficult question to answer in small space. My own convictions have undergone great changes in the past few years; or, to speak more exactly, whereas formerly I never had any real convictions, but merely accepted without examination, and repeated verbally, the beliefs of some other people, I now have earnest convictions of my own. Religion, to my mind, is a much more diffused thing than I used to consider it. I can think of those whose every day is a Sabbath, — whose whole lives are sweetened and purified by the love of God, whose every act glorifies Him and makes the art of living well a little clearer and easier for some one else, who would nevertheless be excluded by the severely Orthodox from a list of Christians because they believe in God's future as well as present mercy; believe that the story of Adam and Eve is a parable, as well as the story of Jonah and some others. It is my belief that in general the more attention we pay to forms and ceremonies, to theology, that purely human structure, the less attention we pay to religion, God's structure. There are, of course, exceptions to this rule. I think of some to-day who are of the straitest sect, who would deem they did wrong to walk with a member of their own family on Sunday afternoon, or to write a letter to a mother on the Sabbath, who are nevertheless lovely characters. With my belief, of course I think that the harness they wear hampers and ties, denying to them that breadth and depth of character which is so forcible in doing good; denies to them the enjoyment of that love and freedom which is the outgrowth of truth; and, of course, I believe that such a harness is of human workmanship, and in no sense divine. In the main, as far as I have seen, there are very few happy families where such a code is in order; very, very few where the result of such rigidity is not most grievous for some of the children; and I must say I have as yet seen very few such households where the servants were won to Christ. You will, of course, conclude that I am in favor of comparatively few forms and ceremonies, and that I think the greater number of even these few should be flexible, and subject to the change demanded by our growing knowledge, — that is, growing if we are keeping abreast of the great waves of theological thought, if we are standing in the stream of light which the Sun of Righteousness is shedding upon us in this age. Some things never will change, and to these we cannot cling too lovingly, — that it is right to be pure, to be unselfish, to be kind, to be diligent and brave in doing our work in this world, — our little or much, according to our strength and gifts, to enlighten and ennoble mankind; and all this for Christ's sake. And if we so live we shall have no need to set our servants lessons in the Catechism, or talk religion to them, to convince them that we are Christians. If we take a human interest in them; if we continually set before them high motives for doing well even the most humble work; if we deal kindly, justly, charitably, honorably, patiently with them, — in short, if we *live* our religion, we have small need to talk it. Do not understand me to disapprove of the 'word fitly spoken.' All I urge is fewer religious words and more religious acts on the part of mistresses in general. I am strongly in favor of letting servants know for whose sake and because of whose love you are trying to do right; but I think that you must win their respect and confidence by your treatment of them before your words will have any good effect."

"Mrs. Hughes, do you believe in family prayers?" asked a Silent Member.

"Yes, for those who delight in such service; but if any of the family are in any way compelled to come, I think the effect is most injurious. I was once spending the summer in a quiet place, and at that time it seemed to be fitting that my nurse and myself should study our Bible lesson together, and we enjoyed it very much. But at another time it might not have been as pleasant to the girl. It is always disastrous to try to force anything of this kind. Two truths have been borne in upon my innermost belief by my experience in life, and engraven there in golden letters, — there cannot be too much love; there cannot be too great liberty. License is not liberty, and foolish fondness is not love; but love — real love — and true liberty can never injure. There are to-day many parents clutching their little reins of authority, at the end of which are children fretting and fuming, checked in their growth, and looking forward to their coming of age. If those parents had but the wisdom to drop the lines and utter merely an occasional word of counsel and a frequent word of love, the children whom they fancy would bound away and leap over some precipice, were they given a moment's freedom, would merely graze in the beautiful pastures which line either side of the journey of life, and would grow in grace as rapidly as a house plant grows in beauty when set out in the soft spring showers and the glad spring sunshine. Liberty is a great principle of good government, and it applies as forcibly to the home as to the nation. Remember this in dealing with both children and servants: what you cannot achieve by moral suasion, with any creature who has a mind, is generally best unachieved. Babies sometimes have to be forced, but older children may be won."

The meeting was rather short this time, as Mrs. Hughes had another engagement, and no one felt like attempting to fill her place. For myself, I thought it was better to have the ladies go home when they did, for I was certain they had been fed all the meat they could digest that time. Indeed, I felt that if they digested half that had been given them, their lives would undergo quite a change for the better.

CHAPTER XV.

HOMES, NOT HOUSES.

I AM not at all sure that Mrs. Hughes had in mind any definite subject for discussion when the ladies gathered. Possibly she had, but I cannot believe it was the one she really took up, for her remarks bore every sign of being extemporaneous. There is such a vast difference between the various styles of conversation! Sometimes, to a chosen few, we evolve a line of thought upon which we have studied so much that our words march forth like a well-drilled troop of soldiers; sometimes we argue, leaping from one point to another, as a chamois leaps from rock to rock, and gaining our summit amid a certain enthusiasm of our physical and mental being, spurred to unexpected and hitherto unattained heights by the quickening influence of other minds. And sometimes — how shall I express it? — sometimes a chord of music, a look upon a dear face, or perhaps some one of life's too common tragedies, will fall upon a sensitive, highly-wrought nature. Those vibrant strings which run betwixt the heart and brain will quiver, and set both organs vibrating, and then it is as if the soul were melted and poured forth. It is a species of talk which can never be written, never repeated. It is born in an instant, and it dies as quickly, save in the stirred hearts of those who listen; there it must always live.

I noticed upon the day of which I am trying to give an account, that the Pale Lady looked paler than usual, sadder too, if possible. Indeed, there was something in her face which arrested my attention, and through my mind there flashed a fear that whatever her work here might be, it was almost accomplished. There were two or three other faces there that day that I thought looked tired, — more than that, discouraged. I know that Mrs. Hughes saw all this in an instant, and that it stirred her heart. For a few moments, while the ladies were gathering, she sat silent and absorbed; then, when all was still, she began with slow speech, and a quiet voice : —

"My heart is very full to-day, and I wish I could speak to you as I feel. I am often moved, when I turn my mind to this common phenomenon of life, — the great that lies in the small. Viewed in one way, nothing could seem more practical, less heroic, more devoid of sentiment, than housekeeping, and carried on as it is by many women, it certainly looks petty; but all this is wrong. When we view it in its true light, when we pierce to the centre, we are almost startled. To-day the past rises in my mind. Perhaps I have given you the impression that after a short period of study I thoroughly mastered my household, and henceforth knew no back-sets or trials. But this would be untrue; for long after I had apparently learned every detail of housekeeping, I was often overwhelmed with such a sense of failure as I cannot express to you, but which your own lives will enable you to understand without the aid of weak words. A woman's work is infinitely harder than a man's, because more comprehensive. Let her be the best of housekeepers, — if she be a wife, if she be a mother, she will still see behind her many failures, and before her many difficult and almost impossible duties. A woman's work involves ethical even more than practical questions. Beyond and above her actual housekeeping there arises in her mind a vision of an ideal housekeeping. She has, perhaps, a perfect ideal, and to this she clings, in hope sometimes, but more often in sorrow, and it may be in despair. It is better to face the truth; no man in this world — this world that is but the threshold of another — is going to fully understand the greatness and beauty of your aspiration, nor the meaning of your failures. My heart is so often stirred within me by these thoughts. I look abroad, and I hear one deed after another called noble. I hear the word 'hero,' and then my eyes turn to some of the humblest and simplest homes in our land; there I see some tired mother-face, and I say, 'heroine.'"

"Do you think, Mrs. Hughes, that a woman can be a heroine in a quiet home?" asked the Pale Lady.

"I know it!" Mrs. Hughes answered, and her face and words fairly glowed, "and God knows it too! Oh, how He looks upon this! How far He sees! A woman has been tried beyond her physical strength. She is impatient with servants, children, and husband; they call her ugly. She had meant to be so different, and she is broken with a sense of failure. But God looks at her and He says, 'You are tired, my child; you have nobly tried and you have won. You do not know it yet, but you have won.' Right in some of the humblest homes of our land there are women whose daily life is one long thought for others, one sacrifice of self. They are, perhaps, impatient at times, despondent, utterly discouraged; but God is watching them, and His hand is full of laurels. Some day they will know all. Some day; some day. I believe that many a woman lies down here to sleep, feeling that her work is all undone, her life a failure, and in that other world, where light is so abundant, she is awakened by the touch of a crown, — a victor's crown. I beg you, dear friends, to think of all this when your hearts are ready to sink within you; believe it with all your souls, and it will bring a calm and lofty peace into your discouraged lives. You are keeping *homes*, not *houses;* do you think of that? To husband, children, and servants your influence goes out continually, and in the next world you shall see the fruits of your work. Do not think of it as small. It is the noblest on earth; there is nothing, I am persuaded, in office, hall, or senate-chamber, which in God's sight can equal this work which is appointed unto woman in her own little home. And it is not always the work itself, it is the fitness of the worker which results in perfection. Look at Christ; I have often thought He only assumed a man's form, because of the greater facility it afforded Him for commingling with all. His nature was that of a strong, noble, loving woman, and I cannot help believing that every such woman can come nearer unto Him in her daily life and work than it is possible for any man to approach. It is the physical, the weak, tired physical alone, which gives the impression of failure. Remember that. Often when you think you are lacking in skill you are simply lacking in sleep; often when you think you need more patience, more virtue of every kind, you only need rest. It is pleasant, more than that, it is helpful and stimulating, to receive an appreciative sympathy from those for whom one toils; but do not live upon the hope of this, for it will often be withheld. And do not let this denial break you. Look up, when there is nothing of encouragement below,—look up, and you will see tender eyes and outstretched arms; such pity, sympathy; such marvellous, perfect understanding and love leaning down to you from out of heaven. 'Be ye strong therefore, and let not your hands be weak, for your work shall be rewarded.' Remember that. Forget all else if you will, but oh, remember that!"

The Pale Lady's face was very white, but her eyes were tearless. She sat there, listening quietly, with that strange look that seemed to me born in another world. I contrasted her face, on this day, with that which she had worn during the first meetings of the Club,—that listless, indifferent face,—and I was moved as I began to realize something of what Dolly's Club had done for her. Surely here was an instance of that phenomenon of life,—the great contained within the small. I glanced from one to another of the ladies, and saw a deep interest pictured on every face. My Sprightly Friend seemed quite changed, for her gayety had vanished, and as she listened to Mrs. Hughes's tender words she quietly wiped her tears away. "I dare say," I thought to myself, "she has had her trials, for all she usually seems so merry; her husband is a hot-tempered fellow, and I've no doubt he has often been unkind and unjust to her." Just then I glanced at my little woman. In all my life I don't think that I ever before had quite such a sensation — Dolly was crying!

I am ashamed to say that I felt a hot wave of resentment flash over me. I had not, perhaps, been a model husband, but I was a pretty good sort of fellow, and I felt in a manner irritated and wronged by Dolly's tears.

The meeting was a brief, quiet one that day. No one seemed to feel like talking when Mrs. Hughes finished. I suppose it is seldom or never that women can talk freely of those things which most deeply affect and influence their lives, for they must be fearful that they will let fall the curtain that conceals some one of the many skeletons of which most houses have their share. And so they chatter of the nothings of their existence; but when the great themes are touched they withdraw within themselves and keep silent, and some of them, — yes, I have seen it, — some of them creep away like wounded deer. And so I knew that their silence, on the day of which I am writing, grew out of no lack of interest, but rather the reverse. Indeed, I am certain that at no time since the forming of the Club had the impression of any meeting been as deep. As for myself, I did not meet Dolly, as was my custom, after the ladies had dispersed, to have our usual chat over what was said, and my report thereof. Instead, I took my hat, and going out of a side door left the house. I had no errand, nor any particular intent, other than to avoid talking with Dolly for a time. But as I walked, my feet led me as usual to the path along the lake. I can readily understand that there is truth in the assertion that the Alps have had no little share in the formation of Swiss character, for I have so often experienced the impossibility of harboring petty thoughts in the presence of Nature's grandeur. That day the lake was still, albeit it was shaded by a cloud. Far away it stretched, and with it my thoughts expanded, ran backward, far backward, and forward, perhaps not so far, for I thought of Death, — and who knows how near he may stand at any time? I turned me to the past, and one scene after another recurred to me. I saw Dolly's face. Once it was tired. I came home and found her so; she spoke impatiently to me when I threw my overcoat down in the parlor, and I called her cross, and she burst into tears and left the room. I was too proud to seek her and learn the trouble, and then say I was sorry. Oh that miserable, contemptible pride, which prevents us from saying we are sorry! When I saw Dolly next, she smiled and talked as usual, and I let what I deemed her nonsense pass; but when I thought it all over, I knew better. She was tired; perhaps she had been trying especially, and perhaps things had gone wrong. Many a time when I have come home from my office all out of sorts, Dolly has brightened the fire, as well as her face, and smoothed the entire home for me, till I was won to tell her what had tried me. And as I walked along the lake that day I could feel her soft arms around my neck, and her kisses on my face, and hear her bright, cheerful voice, made soft and tender with love, saying, "Never mind, dear, never mind." Did I comfort her so when she needed help? I could have beaten myself, I felt so miserable, so contemptible! "The weaker sex indeed!" I thought with growing indignation. "How heavily we lean upon them, and how they support and uphold us; and when they turn to us in an hour of need, how we give way beneath their weight, and make them realize that they must stand alone!" Let who will call me a woman! If I am womanly, I am proud of it, and I feel no shame in saying that my eyes became too dim to see the lake that day. Ashamed I am of my pettiness — ay, but not of my sorrow!

A lake breeze had chilled the air before I turned my steps that day, and by the time I reached home it was really cold and raw; so it was comforting to see the glow of our library fire shine from out the window. Right cheerily it burned; and I hurried toward it with an eager feeling which I could scarcely explain to myself, for certainly I was not cold after my long, rapid walk. I saw Dolly, my household fairy, my cricket on the hearth, moving about the room in that way she had, so still and yet so buoyant. I have never seen any other woman who conveyed just that impression of strength, affection, and good cheer, by her mere presence. Dolly was my ideal of the union of brightness, courage, and gentleness. Had I ever told her so? No! How many things we men forget to say, or think it not worth while, or perchance fancy will be taken for granted! Do we fancy that our displeasure will be taken for granted? No! We never fail to speak of that. I was out of patience with my clumsy, blundering sex that night, and I hurried forward with but one object in my mind, and that the opposite of the object with which I had left home. I am not an impulsive man, else I think I should have clasped my little woman in my arms as soon as she opened the door for me. Instead of that, I did not even speak, but hung up my hat in silence, and walking into the library took a seat before those cheery logs. Dolly must have seen by my face and manner that something was the matter, but she had learned by experience not to seem to notice my moods. Oh, how much managing we beasts require! It is degrading to think of it! I looked into the heart of the fire, trying to speak but failing every time, Dolly the while moving deftly about the room and setting everything in order. How many of her little touches went to make up the beauty of our home! At last, as she was passing me, I reached out and took her hand. She turned instantly, and laying her other hand upon my head, said in her loving voice, —

"Dearie!"

"Dolly," I said, — and I think the word must have been almost a sob, — "have I made you feel badly? Have you ever fancied I did n't appreciate your efforts; that I did n't think you did nobly for me? Dolly!" and Dolly bent over me, but what she said I cannot repeat. There are words too precious, too sacred for any hearer but the one to whom they are whispered; there are scenes too holy for any painting. But I can say that as I sat before our library fire that night, with my wife's hand in mine, I turned over a leaf in my book of life, and never will I re-turn it unless my manhood deserts me.

CHAPTER XVI.

SERVANTS' TABLES, WITH AN INTERRUPTION.

"MRS. HUGHES," said the Imitation Millionnaire, when the ladies were assembled once more, "I don't think you have said anything about a servants' table as yet. I suppose, of course, though, you don't let them eat in the dining-room."

"No, not at my own table; but when I lived in a very small house, and before I felt able to buy a gasoline range, my kitchen was very hot in the summer, and I used to feel it was wrong to compel my servants to sit down and eat in such an atmosphere, so I had to let them lift their little table, after it was set, right into my dining-room, and eat there. I never could understand how persons of refinement could allow servants to come right to their table and use the same table-cloth. On the other hand, I think that most servants have great cause to complain of the way they are served in this respect. If they eat in the kitchen, they rarely have a separate table for that purpose, and still more rarely have any suitable dishes. I have always taken great pains to furnish my servants' table as completely as my own, though of course more plainly. I bought them table-cloths, napkins, knives and forks and spoons (which I required them to keep separate from the cooking utensils), spoonholder, vegetable-dishes, platter, carving knife and fork."

"Did they make use of all these things?" asked a Silent Member, with a peculiar expression of countenance.

"Yes, but not without some trouble on my part. I know what you mean; and it is undoubtedly true that servants will complain because of the absence of some things which, when furnished, they will not take the trouble to use. But we must also look at this fact: if a servant has only a few hurried moments in which to eat her dinner, and is all tired out at that, and if her kitchen is filled with soiled dishes, she will naturally clear a little space on the nearest table, and eat a sort of picnic meal. So I found that, in addition to furnishing the outfit, I must furnish the time to use it properly. Matters in this respect moved but haltingly, until I had kept house two years. At that time I moved into another house and laid down some new rules. The immediate cause of these rules was, that I had been much annoyed by my servants eating little fancy dishes which I felt belonged only to the family. For instance, sometimes my husband would order a little cake and cream in the evening. The next day, at luncheon, he would ask for some of the cake, and when I made inquiry of the waitress, I would learn that it was all gone. Bananas they sometimes ate for breakfast; in fact, it became almost impossible for me to keep any little dainty article of food in the house and have the benefit of it. So I determined to make a great change. We have dined at night almost all our married life, and so I set half-past twelve as the hour for the servants' dinner. I gave regular orders for this meal, always allowing them to choose the kind of meat, though I told them I did n't really desire to have them select quail on toast. With this meat I always ordered two kinds of vegetables, also consulting their taste in this respect. Then sometimes I provided some plain pickles, or buttermilk; and as they always had a nice soup for their first course, they had a good dinner. The hour for their breakfast was quarter before seven, and the main articles of their meal were oatmeal, coffee, bread and butter. This was varied occasionally by potatoes and eggs (cooked in different ways), and also by chipped beef, or some little hash, perhaps. Their supper was usually taken at half-past six, and was very simple; tea, baked apples or some plain jam, and bread and butter, being the usual bill of fare, though sometimes they had a bit of cheese or toast,—something a little different. For their Sunday dinner they always had a dessert,—some simple kind of pudding or pie. Our own hours for meals were half-past seven for breakfast, quarter-past one for luncheon, and six for dinner."

"I don't think my servants would put up with such an arrangement," said the Imitation Millionnaire.

"I had one girl who murmured a little, but only one. I always gave my reasons to them. I told them that instead of gathering up what was left from the family dinner, they had their separate dishes, could sit down and enjoy a quiet, undisturbed meal, lasting half an hour or more, and could have their food freshly cooked, and hot from the stove. As to the difference of the fare, I said that their appetites were more vigorous than ours, and their work being more physical than mental, they needed different nourishment. I assured them that if ever they suffered from any lack of good, plain, nicely-cooked food, it would be their fault, not mine, for I would provide them with every opportunity to set a good, inviting table. As for the desserts and knick-knacks which we occasionally had, I told them they were mere luxuries, really unsuitable for their needs, and that if I must provide such things for my entire family, if for any, we should all have to go without, for they were too expensive to be eaten in quantities. My servants have not only submitted to this arrangement, but really enjoyed it much more."

"How did you manage to give your nurse an uninterrupted dinner-time?" asked Dolly.

"I could not always do this when my baby was very young, although I generally managed it so; but as soon as the baby was a few months old we arranged to have his hour for a nap come at the nurse's dinner-time."

"How about the soups you spoke of?" asked a Silent Member. "I remember you once said you always began your own dinner with soup for the first course."

"Yes; I always had enough made at night to serve also for the servants' dinner the next day. Anything of that kind was not injured by warming over, and then in other respects it was fitted for such division. But most of the dishes were generally kept separate. For instance, I never furnished anything like chickens for the kitchen, except upon state occasions; even our roasts and cutlets were kept for our own table. Generally the servants chose pork in some form, or liver, or sausage, all of which we never ate. And when they had a roast or chops it was kept just for their own table."

"How did you manage, Mrs. Hughes, about dinner when your children went to school? We have to have our dinner at just your servants' hour, on their account," said another Silent Member.

"My children are only beginning to go to school now, and they are nearly grown. But if I were forced to have my dinner at that time, I would still try to give my servants a separate hour and bill of fare, but of course it would be much more difficult to do so. We generally dined at half-past one or at two in the summer, until we had a gasoline range, because the stove heated the servants' room to such a degree that it was uninhabitable for them at night if we had a fire in the kitchen in the afternoon. So if we had dinner at night during the hot weather it was all cold. I remember a month when I taxed my ingenuity each day to think of different dishes that were nice when served cold. There really are quite a number, — roast lamb with mint sauce, mutton, beef, veal loaf, jellied chicken, Saratoga potatoes, green peas boiled with mint (English-fashion), beets, lettuce, tomatoes, salads, and indeed many others. All these we prepared early in the day, and then we let the fire go out.

But I never rested until I acquired two comforts for my servants, — a gasoline range and a dining-room."

"A dining-room!" cried the Imitation Millionnaire, forgetting her elegance and her manners.

"I should call it a sitting-room also, I suppose. I mean a room near the kitchen, in which the servants could have their meals, and in which they could sit when not working, and receive their company. I furnished this simply but prettily, — ingrain carpet, little pictures and ornaments on the walls, a few books on a shelf, a table, comfortable chairs of course, and a few flowers. If I were to speak of that room in a purely selfish way, I should call it an excellent investment; but there is a higher view to be taken of life than the moneyed one, and there are purer motives than those which turn merely on selfish pivots. You may think I am a trifle foolish, but I assure you that when I had finished fitting up that room I felt the warmth and sunshine of God's smile on my heart. I let my servants help me in the work, — let them bring out their little treasures, their pictures of the home folks, their little fancy articles received on different Christmas-days; and the delight they took in all this, and the eagerness with which they watched me and stood ready to be guided in matters of taste by my opinion, touched me deeply."

"That was very nice, Mrs. Hughes; but not everybody could afford to do so," said the Practical Person.

"No, that is true; but I think there are many who could afford it if they wished. At the time I fitted up that room I was far from rich. My house was of fair size, but was very plainly though prettily furnished. The only sofa in my parlor was a pine box I had upholstered myself, and other things were in keeping; my dress was of the simplest — tasty, I hope, but very plain. In our home we had engravings, books, and little fancy articles I had made, and we thought it all very beautiful, and we were very, very happy; but it was all extremely simple. We never had a large family; we did not think that was best, or even right. Three children are all we have ever had, and our youngest was not born until we were quite well established, so that even before we began to receive an income from my painting, we lived very comfortably, without undue anxiety, and I trust we were able to contribute our mite toward helping others."

"I wonder, Mrs. Hughes," said Dolly, "if you do not feel that that charity which should begin at home ought to do something such as you have described, for the servants."

"Yes, I do. I cannot help believing that in God's sight they are as worthy objects as any of those whom we take up in the outside world."

"I suppose your servants had palatial bedrooms," said the Sprightly Lady.

"Hardly that, for I should not be likely to give them anything so much better than my own; but they always had a comfortable, well-furnished, even pretty room, provided with closet, bureau, and a wash-stand furnished with toilet-set and foot-tub,—everything necessary for the keeping of their persons and clothes in order. I took great pains to see that this room was warm in winter and as cool as possible in summer. I once lived in a very cold climate, and I found that many respectable families, who doubtless called themselves Christian, furnished no heat for the servant's bedroom,—that, too, when this room was her only place for sitting, excepting the kitchen. I have even known people to add parsimony to inhumanity, and begrudge their servants even the kitchen fire in the evening, expecting them to go to bed as soon as their work was ended. I have no words for such people; but I confess that it is a satisfaction to me to believe that such treatment does not escape God's notice."

"But, Mrs. Hughes," objected the Practical

Person, "some girls are so common and rough, it does not seem worth while to try to do anything for them."

"I know that is so with many; and for that matter, most servants have very immature ideas on the subject of order and cleanliness; but I think it is our duty to strive to improve them in this respect; to surround them with comfortable, pretty furniture, and compel them to take care of it. Such training cannot fail to have a good moral effect. I have often heard people make remarks of this kind, when fitting up a servants' room, 'Oh, I'll just get a husk mattress, it is good enough for those things!' Women who take this low view of their servants will generally have low servants to deal with."

"Still, Mrs. Hughes," persisted the Practical Person, "I think it does not pay to treat all of these girls so well. Many of them are so ungrateful, that after you have done everything for them they will suddenly take offence and walk off and leave you in the lurch."

"I hardly think they will, if the good treatment of which you speak has been judicious. I have rarely had that experience with them, and I have kept house for many years. But even if there is such a chance, I think we should disregard it. Surely we are high-minded enough to wish to do right by our servants, because it is right, and not because they will repay us for good treatment."

"Alas! I fear everybody has not climbed to that high moral plane. I know I often feel as if I needed a friendly boost to help me up there," said the Sprightly Lady.

"Possibly there are mistresses who need to be incited by the hope of reward, just as we have to incite children. Some years ago, one of my children disliked his bath, and cried over it. So I used to offer him some extra fruit with his breakfast if he would go through the trying ordeal without a murmur. I remember his asking his nurse one morning what he was to have for that breakfast if he did n't cry. And she answered that he must be good anyhow, and not just because he was going to get something. I was much pleased that she took such a view of the case; nevertheless, I told her that the moral sense in little children was very weak, and that we first had to incite them to good conduct by making such conduct profitable to them; then when they were older grown, and stronger morally, we could appeal to higher motives."

"That reminds me," said Dolly, "of an article I lately read in the 'North American Review.' It was entitled 'Practical Penology,' and it strongly advocated dealing with criminals as you dealt with your children, — letting them see that it paid to be good, and that suffering inevitably follows wrong-doing. This article described the Folsom State Prison, in California, in which the worst behaved and the least industrious prisoners are fed at the worst table, and those who are more correct and industrious fare better as regards what they have to eat, — the best table being occupied by the best men. In dismissing a man, when his term of imprisonment has expired, the warden impresses on his mind the fact that the outer world is much like the prison; certain comforts and privileges in life being reserved for those who work and obey the laws."

"Such a system, I think, would result much better," said Mrs. Hughes, "than any attempt to use merely moral motives with those who are as ignorant as most prisoners are. The moral need not be wholly omitted, it seems to me, but it should be driven home by the practical motive. For those mistresses who have not yet attained the moral strength necessary to doing right by their servants, whether they are rewarded or not, I would like to say that my own experience and the experience of many others proves that in the long run kind and judicious treatment of servants pays excellently well. And certainly we are in need of some paying investments of this kind. When I look abroad over our land and see the wide-spread trouble that mistresses are having with their service, I feel that it is time we took the matter in hand. I am filled with grief when I think of the great and disastrous effect this trouble has upon our women — our nation. Some ten years ago a friend of mine went to England to fill an important educational position, and she wrote me of the remarkable difference in that intelligence which comes from reading, from keeping posted on the topics of the day, which she noticed between the English and American woman; and this difference she attributed mainly to the comparative permanency of service in England. No doubt it has a great effect. Reading, study, thought, all must have quiet of mind and body; they fly before confusion, haste, or excitement. Now, such quiet is impossible to a housekeeper whose time is liable to be broken up, and her entire household arrangements upset, every little while, by the loss of one servant and the training of another. I apprehend we would have better and more intelligent mothers, and consequently a finer race, but for these servant troubles. The question, then, is by no means unimportant, since great issues are dependent upon its successful solving. Nor do I consider that solving a hopeless task, by any means. I am more and more convinced that the main fault, in this trouble, lies at the mistress's door, and the main remedy in her hands. Let us reform ourselves, and we shall find that we have gone more than half-way toward reforming our servants."

Just at this point one of our maids appeared at the parlor door, but before she had time to speak, the Pale Lady's little boy burst into the room, and running to his mother, sobbed out, —

"Mamma! mamma! come home! Papa's so sick!"

There was a slight change on the Pale Lady's face, as she instantly rose to go with the child. She could not well turn any paler than she was already; it was not that I noticed, but an expression of self-control, of strength, and even of support, that I had never seen her wear before. Dolly immediately offered to accompany her, and somewhat to my surprise the offer was accepted. All the other ladies rose as these two left, and after a few quiet words dispersed.

I took a book and endeavored to pass the time until Dolly's return, but I found myself unable to fix my mind upon what I read. I confess that the Pale Lady had taken a strong hold upon my interest and sympathies, and at this critical juncture I was busy with speculations as to what particular experience she was about to pass through. That this would in some way prove a turn in her lane, I felt confident.

It was over an hour before Dolly appeared, and for a short time after coming into the house she was unable to tell me anything, so deeply moved was she by what she had seen. At last I asked the question I was really eager to have answered, —

"Is he very ill?"

"Yes," she said, "he is very ill; but, Griff," she added with a sob, "they love each other, — they really do."

That last might not have seemed strange to many hearers, referring as it did to husband and wife; but I confess it astonished me, and still more, I confess that I felt some inward doubt about it until Dolly had sufficiently recovered herself to say more.

The poor man, she told me, was completely broken down; she never saw any one more so. For a long time, it appeared, he had been toiling hard in his business, under a great pressure of anxiety, and now, just as he began to see the dawn, he had given way. He had been found by a business friend lying insensible on the floor of his office, and so carried home. Dolly said that when she and the Pale Lady went into the house he was on the sofa, attended by one of the gentlemen who had rode home with him. His wife crossed the room quickly and softly, and knelt beside him; and Dolly's sobs broke forth again as she told me how feebly and pitifully he held out his arms to her and said, —

"Millie! Millie! I'm done for now! I shall always be a burden to you!"

And then they learned that his lower limbs were both paralyzed.

Dolly told me how the wife soothed and comforted him.

"You will scarcely credit me, Griff, but if you could have seen her face, — if you could have seen them both, — you would have known they loved each other. I crept out of the room, for I felt I had no right to stay."

I think that few things in my life have ever impressed so forcibly upon my mind the strength of the tie that binds husband and wife, as what Dolly told me that day. These two in by-gone years had doubtless rejoiced together over that first cry, that wonderful cry, that thrills the very soul and tells a young father and mother that they — *they* have a little child; these two had sobbed together over a tiny coffin, had watched together through solemn, awful night-hours, beside a life that was passing out of this world into the next; these two were joined by that holy bond of a grief which God alone could fully share. And though the years had dragged on, and coldness and petulance had divided them, these things lay deep in their hearts, and the hour of calamity had proved a resurrection-day.

Dolly had lingered about the house some time, although, as she told me, there was not much for her to do just then. I felt sure, however, that she had done much, nevertheless, — soothing the children, doubtless, reassuring the servants, and setting in motion the household machinery that had been checked by the master's fall. The doctor had arrived shortly after the Pale Lady's return, and had assisted to move the sick man to his room; but Dolly had left him there, and did not know as yet what he thought of his patient's condition. That it was very serious, any one could see; and as to the end, no one could foretell that with certainty.

"Dolly," I said, — for my mind was now revolving practical questions, — "have you any idea of the condition there financially?"

"Not the least; but Mrs. Hughes is over there now, and if there is anything of that kind to be spoken of she will know just how to deal with it."

I learned afterward that this subject was not touched upon that night, but that, won by Mrs. Hughes's gentle sympathy and understanding, the Pale Lady talked quite freely the next day, and said they had every prospect of comparative comfort regarding money matters in the fall, but that during the summer her husband's earnings from month to month were their sole reliance. During his illness a little something would still come to them from the office, but it would be too small a sum for their support, and she must in some way add to the income.

For several days Dolly and Mrs. Hughes were in almost constant consultation, and I had the honor to be frequently called upon by them. Meanwhile the sick man's condition underwent but little change. It was impossible, the doctor said, to foretell the end. The nervous system had been greatly overtaxed, and for this reason health, if it ever returned, would come very slowly. For the present there was much, though not immediate, danger of death. To rebuild the system was necessary, and one of the first essentials was perfect quiet of mind and body. The latter was easily enough obtained, but the former was a more difficult matter; for although the sick man was most of the time in a semi-unconscious state, there were hours when his mind was quite clear, and then he was disposed to worry over his helpless condition and over his wife's pecuniary strait. So we all felt that something must be done at once to set his mind at ease. It puzzled me, I must confess, to try to think of some way in which the Pale Lady could earn money. It would in no wise have relieved her husband or herself to give them anything; on the contrary, that would only have added to their distress. The Sprightly Lady had joined our counsels, and it was she and Dolly who helped us out of this dilemma at last.

"She can sew!" Dolly exclaimed one day; "she is a beautiful seamstress; she can give sewing-lessons. We'll get her up a class."

"And she can dance, too!" exclaimed the Sprightly Lady. "It seems like a poor time for dancing, I know, but she can dance to good effect. We'll get her up a dancing-class, — she can have both."

It did seem a little inappropriate at first, but we all remembered that the Pale Lady had been a beautiful dancer in her youth, that she was remarkably graceful now; and even if, in her sad married life, she had forgotten much of this art, she could easily recall it. For several days Dolly, Mrs. Hughes, and the Sprightly Lady did little else than drive around — not together, but separately — in search of pupils for the Pale Lady. They were aided in their efforts by all the members of the Club, and indeed some others, — for a few of my gentleman friends and myself did what little we could. Of course they first made known their plans to the Pale Lady herself, and she gave a ready and grateful consent to teach the classes if they were formed. At the end of a week the ladies had the pleasure of announcing to her that two classes, one of twenty-six and another of twenty-eight pupils, were ready for her. Her income from these would be something over thirty-five dollars a week, which would place her beyond all occasion for anxiety; and although she would have to give up four mornings every week to the work, she could, with good servants, she said, so manage as to spare the time without much trouble. She was further relieved by having her three little children taken by friends who would care for them tenderly. Dolly brought one to our home, and Mrs. Hughes wished to take the other two; but the Sprightly Lady insisted upon dividing this pleasure with her. Every day they were taken to see their mother; and although she doubtless missed them sorely, their absence must have been a great relief in some ways, since it lessened her cares, and enabled her to maintain throughout the house the perfect quiet their father needed. Of course she went out to her classes, — one of them meeting at Mrs. Hughes's, and the other at the house of another friend whose parlors were large. I really think these classes were of great benefit to the Pale

Lady in other than a financial sense; they seemed to rouse her interest, her spirit, — in a manner to renew her youth. She was indeed a beautiful seamstress. It is a pity that all ladies are not the same, for nice sewing is such a refined, ladylike accomplishment. The pupils were taught not how to embroider with Arecene and Kensington stitch, — many of them knew that already, — but how to hem daintily, fell exquisitely, and darn so that the rent became almost an ornament.

With her other class, too, the Pale Lady succeeded entirely. Of course many new steps and dances had been introduced since her youth, but it cost her no effort to learn all these, for dancing was as natural to her as breathing.

I never knew what her husband said with regard to her taking the support of the family upon herself; it was, of course, contrary to his old ideas and theories for a woman to be self-reliant; but I have the belief and the hope that many of those old ideas and theories were shattered the day he fell so heavily on his office floor. Life is a queer thing: it has ways of convincing a man, and it has ways of ridding him of a belief.

It was manifest to all who entered the Pale Lady's house, that a great change had taken place in its management in the last three months; and I think Dolly was fully justified in attributing this change to the influence of the Club.

"Griff," she said, one day after we had been talking of the sick man, "it seems a little strange to think how he is now taking the benefit of what he not only never aided but would have done his utmost to defeat, had he known of it. But I suppose we all do more or less of that, — receive benefit from what we have never helped along."

"Yes, I suppose so, though the thought is humiliating. Many do that in religion, — throw ridicule upon it at the same time they are greedily living on its benefits. It's pretty small, is it not? We are like children, — too ignorant to know what's for our best good; and we sometimes put out the fire that would have warmed us, because we fancy it is needless or dangerous."

CHAPTER XVII.

SIMPLIFYING LIFE.

THE Club missed its meeting one week, because the more prominent members were fully occupied with their efforts to help the Pale Lady through her trouble. But the next week it met as usual, and to every one's surprise the Pale Lady herself was present.

"These discussions have done so much for me," she said quietly, "I could n't forego them; and then," she added with a deep flush of pleasure, — the first flush I had seen on her face for years, — "my husband urged me to come."

As the ladies were chatting a little on various subjects preparatory to the opening of the meeting, I was thinking of Mrs. Hughes's last week's work. Some had been so blind and ignorant as to call her selfish and cynical, because she spoke against the fashion of making and receiving calls, as was common among ladies, and refused to indulge in it herself. But all who were really acquainted with her were well aware of the fact that the moment she knew of any persons in trouble she was by their side if possible. She seemed to look upon the aid she gave as the most simple, natural thing in the world.

"We are all members of the human family," she often said, "and if our brothers or sisters need us, ought we not to rally round them?"

"Mrs. Hughes," said the Practical Person, when the Club was called to order, "I wish you would please make it clearer to us how you have managed to find time for so many different things."

"One reason is, I think, that I have simplified life as much as possible. As the world grows in size and knowledge, work is both diminished and increased; much of this increase we cannot avoid, but there is much more that we can. Life is too complex, and we must simplify it. I simplified my table, concentrating my chief efforts upon one meal; then I simplified my dress and that of my children; simplified my social duties and pleasures; simplified the care of my children, training them to give as little trouble as possible; and, as I told you once, I heartily believe in simplifying the cares of motherhood, — that is, by having fewer children. Is it not better, far better, and nearer the right, to bring but few children into the world, and to give to those few a good constitution, and that training and education which shall make of them splendid men and women, and at the same time preserve one's own health and be able up to the last to guide and aid these children, rather than to have a large family, some of them feeble, and all more or less lacking in mental and moral training and advantages, and end by being a physical and nervous wreck one's self? I know not what view you take of God, but to me he is our Father, — wise, and just, and kind; and I am sure he never intended any such condition of affairs as now exists, and I am equally sure that in process of time such purification of life and character will take place, that this condition will be supplanted by one far nobler and better. When I hear any woman talk of the inevitable, and of what we must expect, being women, and of this being our lot, and we born to it, and so on, I feel that she has gotten behind her age instead of ahead of it, and is using what little strength she possesses to drag it back to where she stands.

"We all know that life may be made very different in the hands of two different people. I have some dear friends who, albeit they possess fine characteristics, have, as it seems to me, a most mistaken idea of proper living; for they are rushed along so fast with their charities and their social duties that they have scarcely a chance to breathe, much less to think. Their constitutions are overstrained; they are constantly more or less tired, even jaded, and so are those of their household who try to join them in their toils, while others of the family are, owing to their different natures and tastes, repelled, and so perhaps go to the other extreme and do not give their share of aid. Such lives are most unfortunate, it seems to me, for they do violence to the physical being, and utterly destroy that peace and quiet which is the only proper atmosphere for a home, — the only atmosphere in which children can be properly reared and equipped for life. But you can do nothing with such people; they mean well and think they are doing right, and their many estimable traits win your respect in spite of their mistakes. You can only regret that the energies which would accomplish so much if properly directed should be so perverted. If you attempt to talk to them, they will perhaps speak of the pressure, the intensity of the age; will say that this must act on all those who are in their proper place in the rank and file of battle; and then, perhaps, with talk of drones and sponges, they will hurl back your well-meant words against yourself. Such people can scarcely realize that 'they also serve who only stand

and wait;' still less can they realize that those who quietly and steadily pursue a systematic, well-thought-out course in life, will probably in the end accomplish more good without as well as within the family circle than those who run through life at such high rate of speed. There is a chapter in that inspiring little book called 'Our Country,' on intemperance, in which the increase of this vice is — very properly, it seems to me — connected with the increased nervousness of our people, and this nervousness is attributed partly to our hurried mode of life. I am sorry the writer did not go further and urge those who are opposed to intemperance to use their influence against this rapid way of living. I think that although some will disagree with my conclusions, yet all will concede that this subject is of sufficient importance to demand our earnest consideration."

"Don't you think, Mrs. Hughes," said the Practical Person, "that it is important to be systematic if one wishes to accomplish much?"

"Very important, even necessary; but I think that when one is leading such a life as I have spoken of, a system is really out of the question. When our lives are harmonious, when, like a choice conversation, they become a fine selection, they will naturally fall into a well-ordered system. No system can or should be iron-bound; it must be more or less flexible to be of aid; but although changed sometimes, and occasionally abolished for a brief space, yet it should exist none the less. We have heard of students who drop the history right in the middle of a sentence, if perchance the history hour expires just then. But no one would hold up to ridicule those men and women who so judiciously arrange their employments that there is no rush and no waste. A housekeeper's plan of work should include many margins. She will find that, if she arranges to have a certain task ended and another begun at any particular hour, and struggles to carry this out, she will keep herself and her household in a temper the reverse of angelic. Leave plenty of time for incidentals, and you will generally come out even."

"But, Mrs. Hughes," urged the Practical Person, "I think this is impossible, unless one has enough help to do the work."

"Certainly; it is just as impossible as it is to keep a house in order if one has no places to put various articles. But many people who have servants are so lacking in system that they do not properly arrange and order the work, and it is always behind. The consciousness of being in arrears is more fatiguing than the work itself.

Some people have by nature more of this quality — this capacity for arrangement, coupled with executive ability — than others; but I think that even those who are lacking could cultivate something of it. Without it they can never be successful housekeepers; indeed, they cannot live successfully. I know a lady who has but one child and boards, who often laments her lack of time, and says she cannot conceive where it goes. But her conclusion always is that those people who have more duties than she, and yet enjoy more leisure, must neglect something. Of course, such a conclusion is very comforting to herself, but it is nevertheless erroneous. The reason for such difference is her lack of good management. She wastes time. I know that she performs her few duties no more faithfully than some other friends of mine perform their many. She squanders her capital — time — or lets it run to waste; the others invest it judiciously. If, instead of trying to justify herself, she would conclude that she must be in the wrong, and conscientiously try to find the remedy, the result would be a great improvement in her own life and that of her child. No mother can teach that most important art, the proper management of time, unless she herself practises it.

"I once visited in a household where there was

never time for anything, and by observing I soon discovered many reasons for this. One was the multiplicity of occupations; another the great amount, not of conversation, but of talking, that was done. Two or three members of the family would undertake together to perform some little piece of work to which one could have attended without difficulty, and over this there would be perhaps half an hour wasted in chattering. Now, some people may raise shocked hands, and say that Mrs. Hughes is even opposed to family conversation. I don't think that I am; but most of the talk that takes place as I have described is mere chatter, useless to say the least, and some of it worse than useless. Of course people will continue to so pass their time if they wish; but they should not be surprised if, at the close of their day, they can look with no satisfaction upon what they have accomplished. I also know of a family of great culture and warm affections, where the custom is for the various members to meet at the table for a meal, and then disperse for a time in order to engage in different occupations. Much of the day they are as separate as if they were out of the house. When they meet, they have delightful social times."

"Mrs. Hughes," said the Sprightly Lady, "I have heard some say that the trouble with

Carlyle was that he was around too much. You evidently think that some women are around too much also."

"Yes, I do. The various members of a family not only waste a great deal of time, but they also see too much of each other. I think that family intercourse would be more interesting, as well as more valuable, if it were freshened, not only by reading and thought, but also by abstinence. I would not have people get in the habit of maintaining a gloomy silence when together, — few things are more depressing than that, — but I would have them together less frequently; or, if the size of the house did not admit of separation, I would enjoin upon them such active, healthful occupations as would preclude this idle chatter, without giving any impression of gloom. Then, when their duties were ended, or when they sat at table, I would have every member of the household do his best to add to the general interest and happiness. This certainly does not mean making a great noise, or talking everybody else down. If each is ready to take his turn as talker and listener, and, above all, to show an interest — an unselfish interest — in whatever is advanced for common entertainment, he will find his reward in the happiness of such family meetings. Such a household as I have in mind is most delightful, but impossible, I think, for any mother save one of rare qualities."

"Do you think it is possible, Mrs. Hughes," asked one of the Silent Members, "for a woman to direct work that she herself does not understand?"

"Yes; I know of a case where a woman is an excellent housekeeper, albeit she never cooked a dish or did any other housework in her life. She possesses wonderful executive ability and wonderful power of control over others. I do not think her servants are apt to love her, but they certainly obey her. I cannot help believing, however, that more knowledge would improve her, for it does not seem possible that she can rightly sympathize with and understand her servants, when she knows so little of their toils. Certainly it would be unsafe to recommend her ignorance to women in general; for, not possessing her peculiar powers, they might simply succeed in copying her defects."

"Mrs. Hughes," said Dolly, "I have noticed that you continually lay emphasis upon a mistress's understanding her servants' work, and sympathizing with their exertions."

"I think we cannot too often emphasize that point. I know I derive benefit in dealing with my servants by frequently letting my mind dwell upon the hardships of their life. This thought should not incline one to foolish indulgence, but it should temper severity, and should have a strong influence over us,— inducing us to mingle kindness with justice when we deal with them."

"By the way, Mrs. Hughes," said the Sprightly Lady, "a friend of mine remarked the other day that she did not believe there were ten ladies in this city who knew how to be kind to their servants without being familiar with them. I felt that some one ought to fight her on behalf of the city. I suppose the Mayor is the proper person to call her out."

"I am afraid there is some truth in her statement, although I hope her figures are too small. But there is really little to be said on this theme. A peculiar mingling of gentleness, kindness, and dignity belongs to the true lady, and it is as indescribable as inimitable. If one is not to such manner born, she can never possess it, for it is not to be acquired. But to return to the hardships of a servant's life. Some time ago I was reading in an English magazine an article on butchers and their bills. The complaints of many people about the high price of meat were mentioned, and readers were reminded that it was impossible for butchers to buy in larger quantities than their present needs justified, and store away, as could other tradespeople, and so they had to buy for the day, as it were, and gain or lose according to the chances of sale; and buying so, they had to pay a larger price for their stock. But the point in the article that reminded me of the servant question was this: The distasteful features of the butcher's trade were dwelt upon, and the statement made that there were fewer applications for apprenticeship to this business than to any other equally prominent. I immediately thought of our kitchens,— our greasy dishes and soiled clothes; I thought of the summer's heat and the winter's cold. In my mind some sharp contrasts arose: the mistress on the gallery, of a hot day, and the maid over the cook-stove; the family abed and asleep, of a cold winter morning, and the maid trying, with benumbed hands and feet, to start the fires and get the breakfast; and as figures in this picture, I saw my servants with their heated, tired faces, just as I have seen them many a time. And thinking of all this, I assure you I did n't begrudge them any of their pleasures, but rather cast about in my mind to try to discover ways and means of still further lightening their toil and increasing their comforts. It would be well for us mistresses to bear in mind these lines from 'Henry VI.': —

> 'Thus are poor servitors,
> When others sleep upon their quiet beds,
> Constrain'd to watch in darkness, rain, and cold.'"

"Mrs. Hughes," said one of the Silent Members, "what do you think when the lady of the house is obliged to do all this work and to perform the duties of wife and mother in addition?"

"To begin with, I can say that I don't think she can perform the latter if she has the former on her hands, unless her family is very small. But I have already expressed myself upon this point so often, that I fear any words I speak now will only seem to be a repetition; then, too, I feel so strongly upon the subject that I am fearful of speaking with undue heat. To sum it all up, as it were, I earnestly pity such women, and think that most of them married too soon, instead of waiting until the income justified at least a tolerable mode of existence. I think, too, that in the majority of such families there are far too many children. I have often heard people deplore the fact that some of these poor household drudges are without daughters; but, right or wrong, I cannot help feeling a certain pleasure when I see there is no daughter in such a household. I feel that to a certain extent, perhaps only a very limited extent, the mother is responsible for the conditions of her life, and I cannot help rejoicing that there is no young girl there to choose one of three things,— to be an unnatural daughter and refuse to bear her part; to have her young life worn out by the same spiritless, ceaseless drudgery; or to marry into similar evils, probably. I trust you will understand that I am not referring to any reasonable amount of housework, but to overwork, — work in those households where the supply never equals the demand; where the work is always in advance of the worker, and one must continually toil along with no prospect or hope of really getting through. There are many such households, but there ought to be very few. For my part, I can think of but one reason that can justify such a condition of affairs, and that is some long-continued ill-health or calamity which deprives the parents of an income which has been sufficient to justify them in having a family of children. Of course, under such changed circumstances there would have to be an entire change in the mode of life."

"I have two children," said the Sprightly Lady, with a penitent air, "but now I think of it, I am not sure that my income justifies more than one. Would any of you be so kind as to buy Tommy, and take him off my hands?" she added, looking around with a comical air of earnestness.

One of the Silent Members, who had no children, readily offered to take the small Thomas.

"I'll consult Billy about the price, and let you know," said the Sprightly Lady. "And now that this painful matter is disposed of, will you please tell me, Mrs. Hughes, something about gasoline ranges; do you think they are safe?"

"I have found them so. I have used several different makes, and have had one in my house now for some years, and I have never had an accident. Of course I explain the danger to my servants, and caution them to be very careful. Kerosene is dangerous, yet many people trust their servants to handle it; and although we occasionally hear of a fearful accident, such things are rare, considering the amount of oil used. In truth, fire is a most dangerous element, but we have to trust our servants with that. To prevent accidents, we must teach them the danger of carelessness. I should be sorry indeed to give up my gasoline range, and so would my cook. For two years, now, I have used one in winter as well as summer."

"How do you heat your kitchen?" asked the Practical Person.

"I have a base-burner furnace-stove in the servants' hall, as I call their dining and sitting-room, and this heats the kitchen nicely, and by means of a drum, and two hot-air pipes, also heats a bath-room and both of the servants' rooms equally well. It costs no more to run this stove than it would cost to run a coal range, and it adds much to the servants' comfort. These five rooms are warm both night and day. The gasoline range stands in the kitchen, and is only lighted when needed. It is not nearly as expensive as a coal range, as we buy the gasoline by the barrel (which, by the way, we keep in a little shed separate from the house), and it dispenses with all the trouble and dirt of fuel. But," she added, glancing at her watch, " I see it is time to extinguish my conversation, as well as my range."

"Turn out both gases," whispered the Sprightly Lady, less elegantly but more briefly.

CHAPTER XVIII.

ONE THING AT A TIME.

I HAVE so far made but slight mention of a little change that took place in the conduct of the Club soon after its establishment. At first the conversation was more general, Mrs. Hughes bearing not much more than her proportion; but as the interest deepened, and the topics increased in importance, it became the wish of the ladies to have Mrs. Hughes, who was older and more experienced than the others, deliver a series of short lectures on subjects connected with the servant question, these subjects being chosen by the various members of the Club; each lady feeling at liberty to interrupt at her pleasure, and make such comments or ask such questions as she desired. Mrs. Hughes, who was quite ready to do anything that all the rest thought would contribute to the interest and success of the Club, assented to this plan, only asking that the ladies would hand her, at their next meeting, a list of topics upon which they wished her to speak during the coming weeks, such list being, of course, subject to additions from time to time. A few weeks previous to the meeting of which I am now writing, Mrs. Hughes suggested that the ladies should hand in no new topics, unless they had some in mind with which they were particularly anxious to have the Club deal, as she already had on hand almost a sufficient number to occupy attention until the time for the summer vacation.

"At our last meeting," said Mrs. Hughes, when the ladies were ready for the business of the day, " I was asked to tell what means I had used for making the most of my time. I would like to-day, with the ladies' permission, to speak of a point which is closely connected with that subject; and that is, concentration of thought and aim. As I said before, I used to set apart a certain time for the active supervision of my house, another time for my studies, and so on; and I am certain that I derived great benefit from putting my entire mind upon whatever work or pleasure I undertook. If I was painting, I thought only about that, letting all else go; when it was time to drop the painting and take up the household, I turned my undivided attention to bills of fare, orders of supplies, or whatever branch of housekeeping I had at that moment in charge, never giving my painting even the fraction of a thought. I believe that many people weaken their brains by distraction of mind. Even little children should be taught to work while they work and play while they play."

"Don't you think that power of concentration is a natural gift?" asked the Practical Person.

"Sometimes," answered Mrs. Hughes; "but it is very susceptible to cultivation and neglect. I think I probably possessed something of this power in the beginning, but I have always had to cultivate it also. This culture used to be very difficult, and even now it is not always easy; but I am continually conscious of its benefits. I have often left my studio, after struggling with the conception of a piece, feeling very tired, and have gone to my nursery, and giving myself entirely up to my children for half an hour, have returned to the studio quite refreshed. In the same way I have often dropped some worrying household cares and gone out for a brisk walk, thinking the while upon something else, and returned with new zest to the knotty questions. If any one were to ask me what I considered one of the most important recipes for preserving youth and health, I would say, breaking the tension frequently, snapping it off short. You will understand, of course, that I do not advocate running from one thing to another every five minutes. The length of time in which one is able to dwell, without change, upon any particular subject, or engage in any particular toil, varies much with different individuals; but no one is so strong, mentally and nervously, as to be able ardently to pursue any especial occupation for hours, and to carry it into his relaxations, without suffering much injury sooner or later, not to mention the loss sustained by the occupation itself from this too long-continued labor."

"Since we are recurring to past themes, Mrs. Hughes," said the Practical Person, "will you please say something more of what you think about the policy of treating servants well?"

"I confess that this theme is distasteful to me, for it involves so much selfishness and so little nobility; but as this is, in some of its aspects, a selfish world, we must face even such questions. I would most heartily say that, as far as policy is concerned, kindness to servants pays exceeding well."

"Some of my experiences would go to contradict that theory, Mrs. Hughes," said the Imitation Lady. "I am sure I've been as kind as I could be to some girls who have treated me shamefully afterward."

"That is a deplorable experience which most of us have had at some time or other, doubtless;

but we must draw our conclusions from the general average of cases, rather than from isolated instances."

"I think I can testify on Mrs. Hughes's side," said one of those ladies who seldom spoke. "I have sometimes had the most touching returns from my servants for kindness. We've been ill a great deal at our house, and my servants have always stood by me. Last spring, while I was sick in bed, two of my children were taken with scarlet fever. My husband told the servants that there was great danger of contagion, and that they might leave if they wished. They made him no answer, — they are quiet girls, — but turned and went on with their work. We were cut off from everybody and could get no outside help, so their tasks were very heavy. In addition to all the rest of her work, my nurse took her regular watches and cared for my sick little girls."

"It is wonderful she did n't catch the fever," said the Practical Person.

"She did," said the lady. "If she had died I think it would have almost killed me. We took care of her, of course, and fortunately she had it lightly. I shall never forget what she did for me, nor the other girl's service, either; one treasures such things."

"Yes," said Mrs. Hughes, "they hallow life

and keep the heart tender. I have no doubt that all mistresses have at times been touched by the gratitude of their servants, and indeed I have known of many instances where these ignorant girls have treated a thoughtless and really unkind mistress with a magnanimity that should have shamed her. Whenever I have been ill I have leaned upon my servants, and they have never given way. Once, during my own illness, one of my children was made sick by the neglect of a servant. To be sure, it was the neglect of a duty which, when I was well, belonged to me and not to her; but I called her to my room and talked with her seriously about it. I reminded her of the efforts I had always made in her behalf, and told her that now I was quite helpless and needed her kindness and assistance, and that I looked to her, not only to perform her duties faithfully, but also to take my place as far as she could. I cannot begin to tell you how faithfully both she and my cook served me at that time; how much thoughtfulness and forbearance they showed. In my convalescence,— that most trying of all times; that season when the weak nerves are struggling back to life; when you are out of all danger and everybody thinks you are doing well enough, but you yourself know that you are a thousand-fold more in need of tenderness, sympathy, and every form of loving-kindness than ever you were when most ill; that time when you cannot help being unreasonable; when every sound jars upon you, and every act of seeming indifference breaks your heart afresh, — at that time, with me, it was oftenest my servants who showed most sympathy and the truest and most constant kindness."

It was seldom that Mrs. Hughes betrayed emotion, for she had a wonderful power of control; but Dolly saw that this power was severely taxed just at that moment, and immediately claimed the ladies' attention.

"I have not kept house very many years yet," she said, "but I know that most of these servants have kind hearts, and will show their kindness if we but let them. I think they often feel that their mistresses care nothing for them personally, but are merely trying to get what they can out of them; and of course such thoughts are hardening."

"Do you believe in rewarding servants, Mrs. Hughes?" asked the Imitation Millionnaire.

"Not for all they do, perhaps; or, to speak more correctly, I do not believe in turning around and paying a girl for every extra service which she may perform out of kindness of heart. That would be doing her injury and depriving her of the elevation of character which is God's payment for a noble act. But I think that appreciation stimulates virtue; we all crave that, and I never fail to let my servants receive it from me. Such services as we have been mentioning cannot be paid for in dollars and cents; but I think we do both ourselves and our servants a wrong if we do not notice them in some way. It has been my custom for years to make for those servants who had lived with us a long time, or done especially well, a very happy Christmas. We have known seasons when we felt that we could not afford to give each other any present, unless it was some little inexpensive thing we ourselves manufactured; but we have, even at such times, expended considerable on our servants."

"What kind of presents do you make them?" asked Dolly.

"Cabbage and roast pig," said the Sprightly Lady.

"No, not exactly that, but something practical," answered Mrs. Hughes. "When we were quite limited in our means, we used to buy calico gowns, white aprons, handkerchiefs, and so on, for them. Usually we put the various articles into different parcels, so as to have a series of surprises, and gave one from the baby, one from the next child, and perhaps one or two from myself. These presents were on the

Christmas-tree, — for we never failed to have a tree, if it was no more than a twig, and we were all very happy around it. Of late years I have tried to find out from my servants before Christmas what particular gift would be most acceptable, and have added this — an album perhaps, or a shopping-bag — to some more practical articles. There are those who think that a present should always be something superfluous, — something the receiver could not have given himself; and there certainly is wisdom in this, although it would not always be best to be guided by such a rule, for often people are really in need of practical articles, and a present which answered those wants could not fail to be more acceptable than one which took a more romantic form. It is almost needless to say that I think it very wrong to give servants any finery, — anything which would encourage in them tastes unbefitting their condition or means."

"I have the same feeling you have about rewarding servants, Mrs. Hughes," said the Silent Lady who had spoken a few moments before. "After all our illness last spring I went away with the children. I knew our summer was to be very quiet, but I resolved, even before we left, that I would try to make my nurse have a happy time; and I know I succeeded in this. I gave her many little privileges, and took pains that she should see whatever there was to be seen; and as she formed some pleasant acquaintances among her own people, I am sure she enjoyed the summer."

"Virtue is said to be its own reward," said Mrs. Hughes; "but I have noticed that few object to a little something additional, and I think that we may safely conclude that our servants are at least as human as we. To change the subject a little, I would like, if the ladies will excuse the digression, to give a description of a house of which I was lately told. Although foreign to our more recent topics of conversation, and possibly so to our topic proper, — servants, — yet it is closely allied to a subject upon which we have already touched, — that of making a home beautiful upon small means. The house whose description excited my admiration is the home of a married couple who are rich in culture, but whose means are quite limited. Upon the lady's entering the old family mansion as its mistress, she found that it had heretofore been the custom of the household to store in the garret any article of injured furniture. There were a number of old-fashioned pieces living thus in deep and melancholy seclusion, and she had them all carried downstairs, and with some outside assistance put them in perfect order. As some of this furniture was extremely old in style, it is now quite valuable, in a day when the antique is so highly prized. The house itself, although substantial, was rather bleak in its appearance and appointments. With the aid of an ordinary workman this lady made great changes and improvements in the large yard, and within doors she must have transformed the place indeed. She employed a Frenchman who possessed some taste, but no skill beyond that of almost any good common painter, and with his help alone she frescoed the entire house. In her parlor she hung lace curtains, which she had dyed a delicate blue. On the ceiling overhead, pale morning-glories seem to grow and blossom. Pond-lilies in the upper and day-lilies in the lower hall rival the splendor of Solomon. In her husband's study stands a tall palm-tree, and this tree finds like comrades on the walls; while the lotus-flower and other suggestions of Egypt add to the classic beauty of the room. Her own study glows with the warmth of many-shaded reds, and on the walls the coral honeysuckle twines its beautiful lengths. This lady has until lately done but little painting, although of course she must always have been an artist at heart; but in decorating her new home she was, as I have said, assisted by a man who had no claim to such a title. At times he would despair of carrying out her suggestions, though she aided him by models and even by outlining the designs upon the walls. He would sit and mope by the hour, and all her own energy and enthusiasm were taxed to give him heart once more. Then perhaps he would take his brush and work away right manfully, until the next despondent fit seized him."

"But all of us are not artists, Mrs. Hughes," said the Practical Person.

"No; and all of us cannot have such exquisite homes. I only cited this case to show what might be accomplished without much money. Of course this is not the only form of decoration, although it certainly is one that is unusually beautiful."

Some little chat among the ladies ensued at this point, and then Mrs. Hughes said, —

"The summer is now fairly upon us, and it might be well to adjourn the meetings until next fall."

"Lest the discussions," suggested the Sprightly Lady, "may become too heated."

"Yes," laughed Mrs. Hughes, "there certainly would be some danger of that." And then she added, "It might be well to have one more meeting, and in this to sum up as far as possible the results of the seventeen meetings of the Club. Possibly the best mode of doing this would be to hand in a series of resolutions on some of the various topics we have discussed."

This suggestion met with favor, and Mrs. Hughes was requested to draw up the resolutions. This she declined to do, but said that if the ladies would hand her the resolutions sometime during the week, she would gladly endeavor to arrange them in order, and would also add her own contribution. To this the ladies consented; and after some little chat upon other subjects they adjourned until their final meeting, a week later.

When the ladies had all left, I asked Dolly what she thought of our Pale Friend.

"Why, Griff, I confess I 'm astonished," she said, turning a perplexed face toward me. "I was afraid she would be broken down by all her extra cares; and instead of that she looks better than she has since she was married."

"Dolly," I said, "could n't you see that woman was dying, not from overwork, but for the want of a little happiness?"

"That must have been it; and now she 's really happy, she 's doing so much for her family; and I believe she 's happy in her husband, too."

Yes, I felt that Dolly was right. The woman was happy in her husband at last, and he and she did really love each other. He was not yet my ideal of a man, by any means, nor was he one in whose companionship I could have taken great pleasure; but none could deny that he was vastly improved, nor could any one doubt that his wife's dying heart had been refreshed, and her drooping spirit had once more lifted its gentle head, as do the wild flowers after a soft spring rain.

A little love — what will it not accomplish! And when we come to a great, an eternal love, — a love that leaves the ninety and nine and goes out to seek the poor lost sheep, — is not that indeed God's own!

CHAPTER XIX.

SOME GOOD RESOLUTIONS.

AT the accustomed hour the ladies convened for their last meeting before fall, the scribe being modestly secluded, as usual. Only once did this personage issue from his retreat, and that was before the meeting really began. He then sought out Mrs. Hughes, and begged to know why, in most of her remarks, she had used the past tense. She explained that it was not because either her housekeeping or her family were deceased, but because she was trying to recall a period in her married life which would more nearly correspond to that through which the other ladies were passing than would the present, she having been married longer and kept house more years than had any of the rest of the Club. The explanation being satisfactory, the scribe forgave her and withdrew; and shortly after he was once more seated at his desk, the meeting was opened.

In all the preceding meetings considerable order had been observed, and, contrary to my expectation, I must confess, the object for which the Club was formed was constantly kept in view, and the main theme adhered to with remarkable steadfastness of purpose. But upon this last day — possibly because the resolutions were a novelty and called for more promiscuous discussion, and possibly because it was the final meeting of the Club for this season — there was more laxity noticeable among the members. Of this fact, however, I shall take no further notice in my report, merely sifting out what seemed to be of moment, and letting the rest go. It had been my custom all along to take a shorthand report of the proceedings, Dolly assisting me to put it in proper shape when I wrote it out in full, as it was always necessary to make some few omissions and some slight change in the arrangement.

"Now for Bridget," said the Sprightly Lady. "Mrs. Hughes, let us have the resolutions, please."

"With your permission, ladies, I will read all the resolutions first; and then, after we have discussed them, we can vote upon them. These resolutions have been drawn up as was suggested, and almost all the members have contributed something."

Be it resolved, —

1. That as mistresses we will endeavor to perfect our knowledge of all that pertains to good housekeeping.

2. That housekeeping is a science involving a knowledge of human nature, a knowledge of the chemistry of food, economy of time and means, and many other branches of learning, and as such, in all its broadness and its many relationships, we will study it.

3. That we will endeavor, in the management of our households and the conduct of our lives, carefully to observe system as far as is possible.

4. To require from servants who desire to enter our service, recommendations in some thoroughly satisfactory form.

5. To require our servants to wear simple, neat clothing, befitting their means and their position in life.

6. To pay them according to the quality and quantity of the work they perform.

7. To treat them with justice and firmness, tempered with kindness, and also to govern our treatment of them by principles of the strictest honor.

8. To require of them a greater perfection in their service.

9. To provide them with suitable comforts of room and table, and to insist upon their proper care and use of such comforts.

10. To bear constantly in mind the hardships of their lives, and to endeavor to lessen these by granting them all possible judicious privileges.

11. To economize their strength and time as far as

our means will permit, by the use of all good labor-saving machines and contrivances.

12. To insist upon their taking proper care of their persons.

13. To require them to be respectful, quiet, and orderly in their speech and action.

14. To watch over their morals, always endeavoring to foster in them such traits of character as would increase their value as servants, and would also be of advantage to them were they ever to establish homes of their own.

15. To teach them how to economize judiciously, and in all ways to endeavor to make extravagance disgraceful in their eyes.

16. To supply suitable reading for their leisure hours.

17. To endeavor to come to a better understanding of their character, and also of the difficulties of their life, by looking at matters from their standpoint.

18. To encourage them to talk freely of their wishes and grievances, provided they do so in the proper place, at the proper time, and in the proper manner.

19. To endeavor, as far as in our power lies, to simplify our lives and the demands made upon our time and strength.

20. To endeavor to learn from all possible sources, and to improve every way that lies open to us for the increasing of our knowledge and general intelligence.

It was necessary to read the above resolutions several times, both as a whole and in detached portions. The discussion set on foot by the reading was at times most animated, that upon resolution number six being almost vehement, and, strange as it may seem, that upon number nine being scarcely less so. The meeting had been prolonged beyond the usual hour, when the voting began, the ladies taking up the resolutions one by one, and in their proper order. Numbers four, five, eight, and thirteen were unanimously adopted; numbers one, two, three, seven, fourteen, fifteen, sixteen, seventeen, eighteen, and nineteen were carried by a good majority. Number twenty seemed, as far as its sentiment was concerned, to be received with approval by all; but some objected that it did not belong among a set of resolutions of that kind, while others thought it was already incorporated in number two. Those who were in favor of its adoption argued that the broader a woman's general intelligence became, the better fitted her brain would be to grapple with housekeeping problems; they also argued that, while number two included much, it did not necessarily comprehend general intelligence, and after some discussion the resolution was adopted as it stood. Numbers nine, ten, eleven, and twelve passed, but with a smaller majority; while number six barely escaped defeat, its majority being of the same diminutive size as that upon which the scribe was admitted. To do justice to the ladies, however, I must state that one of them remarked that for her part she would be rather glad to see some change and improvement made in the amount of a competent servant's wages, but that she did not control sufficient money to enable her to join in any such movement; and I feel confident that, although they did not say so, one or two of the other ladies occupied the same position.

"I would like to say a few words more upon this subject," said Mrs. Hughes, after the resolutions had lived through the fierce ordeal of the discussion and the voting. "This remark could scarcely be incorporated in the resolutions, but it is, nevertheless, one which I trust will have much weight with you. If you have a good servant, do not spoil her by over-indulgence, but try by judicious and kind treatment to retain her as long as she is willing to give herself to service. A good servant is one of the pillars of household peace and comfort. I think that a strong, competent, faithful servant can hardly be overestimated; she is the very salt of the earth."

"Briny Bridget," murmured the Sprightly Lady.

"Yes," laughed Mrs. Hughes, "she may well be called briny, both for that reason, and also because she generally comes from over the sea."

After this, the conversation became more general, all the ladies expressing their appreciation of the pleasure and profit afforded them by the Club, and also expressing their hope that they would all meet once more in the fall, and continue these or similar discussions. A vote of thanks was then most cordially offered to Dolly for forming the Club, and to Mrs. Hughes for leading it so ably; and soon after this the ladies dispersed.

Dolly's little Club was at an end for the time being, and I sat alone at my desk, busily speculating as to effects. It was seldom that any such enterprise was able to bear so much present and visible fruit as had this Club in the Pale Lady's case; and although hers was the most marked instance of its influence, I was confident that I could also detect traces of its good work in many of the other ladies. I knew that my little woman had learned much that was of great value. The Practical Person had, I fancied, gained a little sentiment to soften and beautify her somewhat hard practicability. I believed that even the Millionnaire had gained a little wisdom; and although the Frivolous Young Woman had departed, and was, anyhow, what the darkies call "mazin po" material to work upon, yet neither she nor any other human creature could be entirely beyond hope. As to the Sprightly Lady, it was more difficult to say much. She was to me a most fascinating, puzzling little woman, — one of those who seldom betray what is going on in the busy heart and brain, rather disguising such work, but all the while, nevertheless, constantly impressing one with the conviction that beneath those merry surface jests there lies much of strength and also much wisdom. I did not doubt that such a character as hers had gained much from such a club. It was my earnest hope, also, that the Silent Ladies had carried away many good seeds. I felt indeed that for much of the fault and hardship of their lives their husbands were responsible, and that these husbands should have been present at the meetings, — to be thrashed I thought, rather fiercely; to be influenced, Dolly would have said, more gently and wisely.

I am reminded just here to explain that I gave to several members of the Club the name of Silent Lady, not because they never spoke, but because their words were somewhat fewer and more diffident than the words of the other ladies.

Yes, the little Club was over for a time. I felt it was an inspiration on Dolly's part, and

I was certain that its apparent end was but a beginning of much that we should not see, but which, nevertheless, many would feel.

Just here I was interrupted by Dolly coming into the library and saying briskly,—

"Next, I think, I must take up the management of husbands."

"Don't!" I exclaimed with a prophetic shiver. "Pray don't exert yourself any further! You need a long rest. I am really concerned for your health."

Dolly laughed, but showed no signs of relenting; whereupon I assured her that in some unconscious moment she must already have accomplished the very important work she proposed. There were times, I averred, of which the present was a notable instance, when I had a decidedly managed feeling.

THE END.

www.ingramcontent.com/pod-product-compliance
Lightning Source LLC
Chambersburg PA
CBHW030815230426
43667CB00008B/1231